CW01649912

PRAYER

pitfalls & possibilities

PRAYER
pitfalls & possibilities

Cecil B. Murphey

HAWTHORN BOOKS, INC.
W. Clement Stone, Publisher
New York

PRAYER: PITFALLS AND POSSIBILITIES

 All inquiries should be addressed to Hawthorn Books, Inc., 260 Madison Avenue, New York, New York 10016. This book was manufactured in the United States of America and published simultaneously in Canada by Prentice-Hall of Canada, Limited, 1870 Birchmount Road, Scarborough, Ontario.

Library of Congress Catalog Card Number: 74-22916
ISBN: 0-8015-6016-0

1 2 3 4 5 6 7 8 9 10

preface

I'm a person who hungers for God, and the book you're about to read shares some of my struggles to satisfy that hunger.

In the early days of my Christian experience, well-meaning friends, evangelists, and writers impressed upon me phrases like "All you need to do is come to Jesus"—"yield your life"—"just surrender everything to God." I'm sure these expressions are true, but no one told me how to *come*, *yield*, and *surrender*.

To grow in grace requires effort and involves failure. Hunger alone is never enough. And living a Christian life is not simple. Life is complex and grows that way more and more. I can't solve all your problems (I can't even solve all my own), but I can share some of the paths I have followed, the failures I have endured, and the successes I have experienced.

This book begins on the premise that you are "sold" on the need for prayer and are seeking ways to enhance your prayer life. There are "good" and "better" prayer methods. Although experience is an excellent teacher, it isn't always the easiest way. By sharing with you some of my successes and failures, I may spare you some of the effort and some of the frustrations and hurts. However, I would like to declare at the beginning that I am not attempting to *prescribe* prayer methods for you—I don't say that my way is the *only* way. I'm only making suggestions. As you read, maintain a flexible stance.

At the end of each chapter, you will find "Suggestions for Study and Practice." These will help you to rethink the material and put it into practical use in your life. The suggestions are designed for your individual use and, beyond this, for occasions of sharing with a friend or for use with an established group.

Group sharing can add to your growth and pleasure. Someone has said, "No one can be a Christian by himself." I sincerely believe we grow only in relationship to other people; we help one another as we grow. For this reason, I recommend that you share this book with others, so that each person may challenge and comfort—and be challenged and comforted.

contents

1

"I'm listening, God..."

"I'm sick of it!" Joe thundered, throwing aside the book on prayer. "They all say the same thing: 'Prayer is talking with God.' 'Prayer is conversation.' 'Prayer is interaction between two beings.' "

"What's wrong with that?" I asked. "Isn't it true?"

"What's wrong is that prayer is *not* two-way. Not for me, at least. I do the *talking* and God does the *listening*."

"Have you ever tried to listen?"

My question surprised even me, for my own prayer life sounded pretty much like Joe's. I talked to God and I believed he heard, but God never spoke to me.

Joe's outburst sent me on a search which revolutionized my placid devotionals.

I consulted books on prayer. Surprisingly, only two mentioned listening. The first relegated listening to a mystical experience reserved for those special saints who devote their lives to meditation. The other, written more than a century ago, used a well-worn illustration: In praying, we talk to God; in reading the Bible, God talks to us (a dictum familiar to Sunday school children).

God does speak through the scriptures, but is this the only way? Has he no direct and immediate contact with us?

I began asking friends, "Does God speak to you? If so, how do you listen?" Most were too embarrassed to answer, and the few replies I received were not satisfying.

New questions arose: To hear God, do we have to have a special kind of temperament—a martyr's selfless devotion? Can ordinary people hear God?

It's clear that in biblical times God communicated with people, making his will known. People received dreams, visions, angelic visitations, prophetic utterances. Why do we, today, hear so little of divine manifestations? Did all miracles and supernatural occurrences cease with the end of the apostolic period? If we modern Christians don't hear God, is it his fault or ours?

The biographies of the saints reveal instance after instance wherein God met them through some singularly divine action—a word, a voice, a feeling. They gladly proclaimed these visitations, while we of the scientific age keep silent about our religious experiences for fear of ridicule. We are so afraid of being branded eccentrics or fanatics, we conceal the most precious aspects of our lives.

Prayer is not a monologue; if it were, we'd be wasting our time and energy. Either God reveals himself and his will to us, or he is no more than Baal.

Elijah mocked the worshipers of Baal. "Where is your God?" he jeered. "Can't he hear you? Is he on a journey?" Elijah served a God who spoke, manifested himself, and acted. Is the God we serve any less?

I believe that God does speak. The question is, do we give him the chance?

I had no more than picked up the phone and managed a "Hello" before Martha launched into an enthusiastic, twenty-minute monologue. Once or twice I squeezed in a "Hmmm" or "I see." In our "conversations" with God, we sometimes don't let him say even that much. With our friends, we're usually considerate conversationalists, recognizing that good communication requires both oral and aural participation. In prayer, however, we just plain monopolize. Yet, if we do all the talking, how can God tell us what he wants us to know?

I'm learning to *communicate* with God. I'm making listening a vital part of my devotional exercise. Usually God speaks to me; sometimes he declines—but that's his privilege. His silence doesn't mean the encounter has been wasted.

One of my warmest friendships was with Paul, a man four decades my senior. Over a period of years, we took many afternoon walks together. Some days we said hardly a word to each other—but, then, our fellowship didn't depend on verbal communication. At times, we "listened" to each other's silence. We found fulfillment in just being together. Sometimes it's like that with God and me.

Listening to God is a skill not easily acquired. I'm still struggling to hear. Jesus said, "My sheep hear my voice—and they follow me." (John 10:27) He might have added, "But sometimes my lambs get confused."

When I arrived in Africa for missionary service, a myriad of dialects impacted upon my ears. In preparation, I had mastered the grammar book and acquired a vocabulary of several hundred words, but now a sentence sounded like one long syllable. When I began working at hearing, my comprehension improved. The distinctive sounds had been there all along, but I had to get my ears in tune.

Part of learning to hear God is learning to keep quiet. We must shut out other sounds: the voice of our troubled mind, whimpers of guilt, tones of worry. A good way is to repeat the boy Samuel's words: "Speak, Lord, for thy servant heareth," then pause and listen.

In recent years, God has spoken to me many times. On one occasion, I was to conduct a memorial service for a charter member of our church. Because I was new in the parish, I'd never met the gentleman. What could I say? Again and again, I asked God to speak through me, but I seemed to get no answer. Then, as I sat at my desk, a thought flashed into my mind: "How do you define a saint?" I toyed with the idea, then turned to God and prayed, "Father, if this is what you are speaking, make me receptive." He did! Words flowed through my mind as I tapped away at the typewriter. Soon the meditation I needed had fallen into place.

After the service, one of the old gentleman's friends said, "You couldn't have said anything more appropriate if you'd known him." This was heartwarming but not surprising. God had spoken; I had listened.

When my family and I had been in Africa three years, bandits broke into our house. Neighbors heard our cries, rushed to our aid, and saved us from bodily injury. For months, the gang continued to operate in our area, and a nearby Roman Catholic missionary was slashed with swords. Because the bandits often returned to places they'd robbed earlier, we feared for our lives. We had no protection; the locks on our doors would scarcely delay them.

Night after night, I lay awake, tossing and turning. At the slightest noise, my muscles tensed. Finally, one night I pleaded with God to help me get needed rest. At that moment, a long-forgotten Bible verse came into my consciousness: "He giveth his beloved sleep."

"Thank you, Lord," I responded. Then I turned over and slept soundly until breakfast. God spoke; I listened.

Have you ever prayed when you were troubled or afraid and then felt a calmness come over you? Just as Jesus quieted the sea's troubled waves ("Peace, be still!"), he also calmed you. You didn't hear the words, but you felt the message.

God speaks when hearts are open and tuned in. Come with faith and expectancy. Think: *God will speak; God will communicate.*

How will God speak? How will you hear his voice? I don't know, specifically, but that's part of the excitement of listening. Let him devise his own system for communicating with you.

The experiences I know best are my own. God speaks to me most frequently through my thoughts. Sometimes he sends a flash of verse, the refrain of a hymn, a reminder of someone for whom I should pray. I'm discovering that God's means for communicating are as unlimited as God himself.

Suggestions for Study and Practice

1. Evaluate yourself as a listener. Put down on paper several sentences describing your strong and weak points. For a few days, observe yourself and see if you're as good as you thought you were. Now try to improve. Swallow the temptation to interrupt. Be sensitive to the tone of the person's voice and his body language as well as the intrinsic meaning of his words. After practicing these good habits, reevaluate your listening capabilities.

2. Using insights gained from the above exercise, practice listening for God. Do you hear him? What difficulties do you encounter?

3. List reasons why you do not listen to God. Maybe, for example, you're too busy. Or you're shackled by doubt.

4. Be prepared to share some of your experiences and observations with someone else or with a group.

2

Dropouts, cop-outs, and victories

Rush, rush, rush from morning till night. Day after day, the same story. . .not enough hours for all that needs doing.

"Something's gotta give," I wail. Most often, what gives is my time to be alone with God.

Of the dozens of books on prayer I've read, the better ones invariably stress the importance of daily, individual prayer time. But I have a complaint: The authors make it sound easy. Each writer, himself an accomplished pray-er (or so it seems), advocates daily meditation for the rest of us without acknowledging we're likely to run into problems.

In principle, you don't have to convince me that a growing Christian prays systematically. In practice, however, I find regularity difficult. I try. Things go well for a while, then I fail and have to start again. Sometimes I get discouraged and a little rebellious. "Look, God," I say, "I'm tired of praying. . . . I'm just plain bored." With this outcry, guilt engulfs me. *How could I have possibly talked to God like that!* Then something inside me says, "Cec, God's big enough to hear your complaints; if you're bored, go ahead and say so."

While stating my complaint ("It's not easy to pray faithfully every day"), I also make my confession ("I never quite make it one hundred percent of the time"). Those admissions are hard ones, because in sermons, books, and personal testimony, we're led to believe that the Christian is always victorious; he either sidesteps the pitfalls or quickly climbs out of them. I've never met anyone quite so victorious, and that's why I am writing this book—to share victories *and failures*.

Undertaking to pray on a daily, systematic basis creates tension in my life. When I hear of a friend's pressing need, or I myself land in a disturbing situation, prayer is no problem. My difficulty arises in praying for the same people—about the same problems—in the same way—day after day.

I've tried all the good rules:

—*Ask specifically.* (Which I do.)

—*Be individual.* (I give myself an "A.")

—*Be honest.* (This I attempt.)

But sometimes I must add,

—*And then be bored.* (Which I am.)

I guess that at one time or another I've tried all recommended methods, from using a prayer list to releasing myself to be led by the Holy Spirit (only to find my mind wandering).

Then Shirley, who was to become my wife, entered the picture. I had been a Christian a few months, whereas she had known Jesus Christ since childhood. She seemed the perfect example. I wanted to live as close to God as she did.

One day Shirley mentioned she spent an hour each day in private worship, divided equally between Bible reading and prayer. Now I knew how I could live a victorious life: I had only to imitate Shirley!

The next morning at six, I prayed as diligently and as faithfully as I could, then peeked at my watch (hoping God wouldn't notice). Only ten minutes had passed! Back to prayer. My second pause came less than five minutes later.

Needless to say, I didn't make it through a whole hour.

My failure made me feel guilty. "You spiritual dropout!" my conscience chided. That unpromising beginning has been followed by many additional failures and some spotty successes. I still haven't achieved total success (and likely never will), but my batting average is improving. And I've learned some things which I recommend to you:

Begin small. This seems simple, but I wish someone had given me that bit of advice. Try two or three minutes a day—enough time to be meaningful, yet not so much you'll run out of steam or become bored. Think of yourself as a spiritual beginner, a person with a small appetite.

Accept failure. This was hard for me. I was helped by a friend who said of his own worship efforts: "I strive for 51 percent accomplishment. Once I've gotten that much, I know I can begin to increase. The first half is the hardest."

Be honest. God knows your heart, so you might as well be honest. I learned a lesson about honesty with God while reading the fascinating novel *Tell No Man* by Adela Rogers St. John. One night I read to within 45 pages of the end. The next day, I found my schedule so tight that I could claim only half an hour for myself. I could either finish reading the book—*or* have my devotional time.

"Lord, I want to finish that book," I said. "I could give you all kinds of other excuses, but we both know I'd be lying. I want to finish reading, and my will is so strong I know I'm going to do it, regardless, but I wanted to talk with you about it."

Later, as I turned the last page I murmured, "Lord, I'm sorry I put the book first. Forgive me. But really, it was meaningful and inspiring, and I'm better for having read it."

Then God spoke to me—not in an audible voice, but through a feeling: "I'm still here. I've not run away or left you." Now I'm not advocating putting other things ahead of prayer; I'm simply admitting that at times we do cop out. We *all* do. We can rationalize and try to fool ourselves, but God understands the weaknesses of human nature. He may even chuckle over our foibles.

Be systematic. Pick a place—any place—where you can

go at approximately the same time each day. I have my devotional time in the morning, but you may find another time more convenient. A regular place and time enhances the devotional habit.

Make sure you're comfortable—but not too comfortable. One of my earliest choices of a setting was the bed—a big mistake. I resolved to awaken and begin the day by lying in bed for a while praying. The very first day, however, I soon succumbed to slumber. "Honey!" Shirley called. "Honey, I thought you were going to pray." I'd thought so, too, but to lie in bed with eyes closed, under warm blankets. . .well, that takes more will power than most mortals can muster.

Avoid rigidity. Unrelenting routine is deadening—and deadly to the devotional habit. Sometimes I begin in prayer, other times in the scriptures. I may spend the whole period in either the one or the other. I do maintain a prayer list, but to keep its use from lapsing into meaningless routine, I sometimes begin at the bottom and work up.

Daily prayer can be an exciting journey with God. Rejoice when it is, and don't be discouraged when humdrum days come along. *God is good for all seasons, all temperaments, and all times.*

Suggestions for Study and Practice

1. Start or revitalize the private prayer habit by first jotting down the various "costs" (getting up earlier or staying up later, persevering, etc.). This way, you'll anticipate some of the problems and will be better prepared to overcome them.

2. Assume a modest goal—perhaps a little more than "half faithfulness." Each week try for a better record.

3. Keep a log (a journal) of your prayer experiences for a few weeks. Record your problems, solutions, successes, failures.

4. Seek out tips from other people on maintaining regularity in devotionals.

5. You may wish to share your experiences and insights with another person or a group.

3

The family that prays together

At midnight the telephone rang and Paula Hutchenson blurted out, "Jeff's in trouble. Can you come over?"

Twenty minutes later, I found Jim and Paula at the kitchen table. Across from them sat their 15-year-old son, mute and shamefaced. With other boys, he had "borrowed" a parked car and taken it for a "joy ride," winding up in juvenile detention.

"Where did we go wrong?" the parents' eyes pleaded, searching mine for an answer.

Most pastors hear this kind of appeal frequently. My heart is pained as I share a family's heartaches. Jim and Paula were good church members; both taught Sunday school—yet their son had gone astray.

We dedicate our children to Jesus Christ. We teach them. Why should anything go wrong? Why *our* children?

It's easy to blame our chaotic world, our degenerating society, or our declining morals. Cultural patterns are being erased, traditions obliterated. And in the midst of it all, the family—once the core of society—is shaking.

Parents exclaim, "I don't understand this hippie generation!" There's also distrust and disappointment at the other end. On a youth program recently, a teen-ager stated, "The older generation thinks our generation is the worst in the world." Another youth complained: "Our folks are old fogies. They don't understand us. They give us clothes, money, education—everything but love."

A mother was heartbroken. Her son was leaving home. "I don't need you now!" he yelled as he packed his suitcase. "When I did need you, I couldn't find you. You were too busy going to parties and having a good time."

I can't diagnose every family's problems, and I wouldn't dare attempt to prescribe a cure-all. But as a parent and a clergyman, I do have one vigorous affirmation to make: The family that prays together stays together. This is a hackneyed phrase, but I can vouch for its truth. Prayer has cemented relationships within my own family. We're not perfect, but we have a lot going for us—trust, understanding, and openness. Too often have I seen the other side—the plight of families where shared prayer is unknown or ignored.

True family prayer promotes warmth and sharing. Parents exemplify their priorities: they put Christ at the center of the household. Time is taken to be a family unit, to be conscious of one another as individuals. Each member becomes involved in the lives of the others.

The scriptures overflow with evidence of family unity based upon togetherness. Joshua, as head of his household, made the decision: "As for me and my house, we will serve the Lord." (Joshua 24:15) Job expressed concern for his children by making offerings and sacrifices for them. (Job 1:1–5) Of Abraham, God says, ". . .for I have chosen him, that he may charge his children and his household after him to keep the way of the Lord by doing righteousness and justice." (Genesis 18:19)

The Jewish nation, at the time of its spiritual zenith, was careful to perpetuate the teachings of God and to inculcate the tenets of the faith, and this was accomplished chiefly by parents instructing their young. In large measure, it was the failure of the Jewish family that brought about the failure of the nation.

Children tend to emulate their parents' example—whether it's good or bad. A person's first and perhaps strongest contact with Jesus Christ and with the believing community comes in the home. If life there contradicts the teachings of the church, how can we expect to produce healthy disciples for Jesus?

A mean, bad-tempered farmer beat his wife, was surly with the children, and was argumentative with his neighbors. One wintry morning as he trudged to the barn through eight inches of snow, he heard a voice behind him: "Look, Daddy! Here I come!" He turned and saw his four-year-old son carefully placing his small feet in his father's tracks. "See, Daddy, I'm following in your footsteps!"

The farmer's heart was warmed, and his eyes were opened. He certainly didn't want the boy to grow up to be the kind of man he was, so he changed!

Consciously or unconsciously, we set examples. If we don't teach our children to pray, read the Bible, and give systematically to God, we teach negatively.

Look at the things we do take seriously. We rarely skip meals. We religiously clean our houses. We don't miss our clubs and social gatherings. The activities in which we participate regularly reflect our values. Then, what about prayer?

One mother responded, "We know we ought to pray together, but—well, we just don't have time. The kids have so many activities going. Last night, our son gulped down his supper and dashed off to scouts, our daughter had a date, and we went to a PTA meeting."

Another parent stated, "We know we should be a praying family, and we intend to start as soon as we get organized a little better."

Still another complained, "We just can't keep the kids quiet long enough to have a devotional time. You can't imagine the pandemonium we have."

A multiplicity of "explanations" can be offered, but they're really excuses. Talking to a busy executive the other day, I said something about his limitations of time. "Yes," he replied, "I'm busy, but I always find time to do the things I really want to get done."

Priority—that's the key to worshiping together.

Establishing daily family prayers isn't a panacea. In our family, we have our differences and disagreements. Yet, each family member knows he is appreciated and respected as a person. Each belongs!

Today, the young and the old often feel at loose ends, belonging no place and to no one. In many instances, their families have tragically failed them.

Begin immediately to have family prayers together. Select a convenient time—whenever everyone is normally available. It's hard to stick with a schedule, granted, but if someone has to be away, you're still a "family." Our family finds after breakfast best. Other families gather in the evening. Find the best time and stay with it.

When the children were quite young, we skipped family worship on Sunday because we would be spending several hours together with other Christians in corporate worship. Later we discontinued family worship on Saturdays, the only day when we can sleep late. Since we are a family of five and we have joint worship five days, we take turns leading.

Experiment with different methods of family prayer. Over the years, we've revamped our sessions. We always pray and read together, and sometimes we sing. We used to read Bible stories and modern translations to the children. Now we each read, in turn, choosing whatever version appeals to us. It's also important to allow children opportunities to pray spontaneously.

A religious educator was asked by a parent, "When should I begin teaching my son about God?"

"How old is he?"

"Nearly five."

"Run home as quickly as you can and get busy," replied the professor. "You've already wasted the five most important years of that child's life!"

Children are never too young to learn about God. Even before they can articulate their faith, they can feel. They can sense love, understanding, and acceptance. In the process, they become acquainted with God on a person-to-person basis.

The scriptures bear witness that God's people are to be praying people and faithful people who teach their children to honor and love God:

> *Train up a child in the way he should go, and when he is old, he will not depart from it.* (Proverbs 22:6)

> *. . .things that we have heard and known, that our fathers have told us. We will not hide them from their children, but tell to the coming generation the glorious deeds of the Lord, and his might. . . .he commanded our fathers to teach to their children; that the next generation might know them, the children yet unborn, and arise and tell them to their children, so that they should set their hope in God, and not forget the works of God. . . .* (Psalm 78:3–4; 5b–7)

Children learn quickly, easily, eagerly. And they learn from us! But *what* do they learn?

Suggestions for Study and Practice

1. Set up a time when the whole family can worship together. Plan to make this a daily event. Determine that only emergencies will interfere.

2. Make notes (mental or written) of pressures which interfere with regular family worship. Discuss these with your family, looking toward minimizing them and/or their adverse effects.

3. Involve the whole family in planning worship experiences in general as well as for specific days. Solicit the ideas of even the youngest, and listen to all suggestions warmly and patiently.

4. In your sharing group, role play two family members discussing the need for a family devotion program. First, have the "parent" be the advocate and the "child" the reluctant one. Then switch and have the child argue for family worship while the parent offers excuses.

5. With a friend or a group, discuss your failures and successes at family worship.

4

Lucky, bewildered, and surprised

Money problems weighed heavily upon Ken. He lay still, not wanting to disturb Doris. The luminous hands of the bedside clock showed 2:43. He couldn't get to sleep; Dan Summers' offer kept running through his mind. It was terribly attractive, but where could he get the five thousand dollars to "buy in"? He didn't have a credit history to support an unsecured loan, and everything he owned was already mortgaged.

"Lord, please help me," he prayed. "I've been faithful. I've lived a Christian witness. The Bible says we shouldn't be slothful in business, and this is my chance to pull off a good deal. Besides, the returns on this investment will permit us to give more to the church."

Ken's prayer may have been sincere, but it was subtly deceptive. He bargained with God. "I've done what you wanted; now you do what I want." Ken was specifying the terms—five thousand dollars in return for his faithfulness.

Few people consciously speak in such bold terms to the Lord, but how often is an ultimatum implied? Instead of accepting Christ's statement that Christians can ask anything in his name, we demand. We try to maneuver God into an "obligation" to answer our requests.

Even in the pursuit of church affairs, we try to pressure God. Arthur, a conscientious pastor, was battling apathy at New Hope Church. To revitalize his congregation, he formed a prayer chain. Continuously from Friday evening through Sunday night, at least two persons were in the church praying. "The more we pray," Arthur asserted, "the more God will answer."

Arthur's motives were pure, but his method was questionable. "If we pray enough, God is bound to answer" is an out-and-out bargaining attempt with the Almighty. A better appeal would be, "The more we pray, the more we prepare ourselves to receive his answers." Prayer does not change God's will; prayer *discovers* his will.

One of Jesus' parables (Luke 18:9–14) illustrates our tendency to bargain. A Pharisee, trained as a teacher of the law, went into the temple to pray. Reliable, religious, and everything else an ecclesiastic ought to be, he used his personal dedication as a bargaining tool with God. Pointing up to his sacrificial living constrained him to point down to the publican's way of life. "I thank you, God, that I am not greedy, dishonest, or immoral like everyone else; I thank you that I am not like that tax collector." (Luke 18:11, TEV) In his own mind, citing his good works would be cause for God to listen.

Perhaps we bargain because we're not sure God is generous enough to want to help. Maybe he's too high and too busy to show compassion for our puny needs unless we convince him we are worthy of divine favor. Instead, we ought to importune God on the basis that he is our loving Father and we are his children.

My son, John Mark, sometimes uses this approach: "Daddy—" he says as he sits beside me for a chat. (Anytime John Mark sits by me longer than three seconds suggests he wants something more than a chat.) "Daddy, do you need your wastebasket emptied again?"

"No, son, it's fine."

"Daddy, I fed the tropical fish this morning. I haven't missed feeding them for two weeks now."

"Hmmm, that's nice."

"And I took out the garbage. Mommy didn't even have to tell me."

He wiggles closer, then says "Da-a-d-dy" so it sounds like a four-syllable word. He wants something and, unsure of himself, parades faithfully rendered duties as a basis for bargaining.

And that's how we sometimes come to the Lord. Lacking assurance, we don't dare make bold, blunt requests; instead, we try to soften God up.

Confidence and assurance are essential to meaningful relationships. Don and Ralph, college freshmen, spoke to our youth group. Don, who sensed impending failure, spent five of his allotted ten minutes apologizing for his limited speaking ability; meanwhile, the young people fidgeted and whispered. Ralph, on the other hand, approached the group in an easy manner and quickly established rapport. His audience responded enthusiastically.

While we can ask with confidence, we should not try to persuade God through boasts or the parading of our virtues.

The Bible tells of a gentile army commander whose servant became ill. Because this military man gave generously to their causes, the Jewish leaders appealed to Christ: "Heal him, Jesus, for he is the servant of the Roman commander."

Before Jesus could refuse, they continued their pressure. "You really ought to do it. This man is the kindest gentile we know. He puts more in our collections than anyone else."

In contrast, the centurian, speaking for himself, said, "Jesus, I'm not even worthy to come close to you or to inconvenience you. You speak the word, and I'll know the deed is done." He believed, and where the Jews' bargaining gained nothing, the officer's faith got the answer: The servant was healed.

We don't like to face such pronouncements as "there is none righteous" and "all have sinned and gone astray." Our predisposition to prove we're the "good guys" shows we don't understand the meaning of grace. Grace means God distributes his blessings freely without consideration of merits or virtues. Grace is God's goodness poured out upon us even when we deserve nothing but his anger and wrath.

In Victor Hugo's *Les Miserables*, Jean Valjean, newly released from prison, receives shelter, food, and kindness from a bishop. This is not grace, but merely basic humaneness.

The next morning Valjean leaves—and so does the bishop's silver. Recaptured by an observant policeman, the culprit is returned to face the cleric. Valjean bows his head, expecting to be remanded to the prison authorities.

"Oh, let that man go," says the kindly priest. "Those candlesticks are a present for my friend." This is grace—the bishop gave freedom and forgiveness in place of deserved punishment.

Even when we understand the principle of grace, we find grace difficult to accept. We want to be obligated to no one. "I don't know how to thank you," we stammer when presented with an unexpected favor. Our immediate thought is to repay, to buy off the gift.

God's grace flows out of his love for us. Because of our human limitations, we cannot formulate a rationale for that love. A theologian once tried by saying, "God, seeing you would choose a godly life, chose you in Christ." But that is not grace, for it would make God the debtor, who merely completes the transaction initiated by a human being. Instead, God is the beginning. He simply loves us. There's no logic to it.

Being amazed at God's love reminds me of Sam and Ann's golden wedding anniversary. Sam said, "Ann has shown only patient kindness and understanding. I'll never understand what she has seen in me to stay with me half a century."

Ann said, "Sam's a brute of a man in size but one of the most tender people in the world. In spite of all my failings, Sam has lavished love on me for fifty years. I'm the luckiest woman alive."

That's how I feel in relation to God: lucky, bewildered, surprised. God loves me and I don't know why!

When we accept God's love, we feel free to come to him anytime. It's as though he has a sign on his door:

Come anytime.
Never closed. Never too busy.

Suggestions for Study and Practice

1. Over the next few days, as you listen to conversations, be on the alert for attempts to bribe or coerce—to bargain. Do you use similar methods? Is bargaining ever appropriate? When?

2. Analyze your prayers. Do they contain elements of bargaining?

3. Ask yourself:
   (a) "Why do I feel I must prove myself worthy to God?"
   (b) "Am I really convinced God wants to help me (and not punish me)?"

4. Each time you find yourself attempting to "sell" yourself to God, say, "Lord, I'm sorry," and start again.

5. A group may find role-playing productive. Let one person stand, representing God. Let another group member offer several sentences of prayer which carry elements of bargaining. Switch roles. Then, as a group, discuss how you felt about what was happening.

5

"Thy will be done"

Wednesday mornings before going to our jobs, five of us used to meet for an hour of fellowship. In one of these sessions, Mel prayed for several persons outside our group: Martin needed a new job; Carrie faced surgery; Joe and Mattie's marriage was on the rocks. After each request, Mel intoned, "And let thy will be done, O Lord."

Mel's formula reminded me of a medicine show I watched when I was seven. I gawked as the gaudily dressed entertainers sang and strutted. Then an elderly man wearing a blue coat with large white buttons leaped to the platform to spiel about a "secret-formula" medicine.

"It cures ulcers, heart trouble, gallstones, rheumatism, migraine headaches, and diabetes," he proclaimed, displaying a green bottle filled with the wondrous elixir.

The huckster's medicine and Mel's "Let thy will be done, O Lord" were alike in that they were supposed to fit every human need.

Mel's invocation has the ring of the committed believer, but is it a praiseworthy device? We can say the magic words "Thy will be done" so glibly that they become meaningless. Some make these words the sum total of their requests, so their prayers have no content. Instead of communication, there is static. When we say "Thy will be done," what should we mean? In seeking the answer, we can consider Jesus' example.

Nowhere is the Lord's humanity more vividly etched than in the account of the Garden of Gethsemane. As a man, he has a mission to accomplish: He is to die on a cross on behalf of mankind. For the past three years, this carpenter from Galilee has preached, rebuked, taught, and exhorted men to seek first the kingdom of God. Indefatigably, he has traveled from town to town with a single message—"repent and believe." Now, near the end of his public ministry, Jesus is a lonely figure kneeling in a garden. The future holds no surprises, for he knows God's ultimate plan. The supreme sacrifice looms before him.

Never does Jesus cry out "I won't"—but neither does he rush toward death. Being human, he struggles. "Surely there must be another way. Father, if possible, provide another solution." But there is none. So, after great anguish, Jesus pleads, "Father. . .but not what I want, but what you want." (Matthew 26:39 TEV) He prays a second time, concluding, "Thy will be done." Then a third time.

Three times Jesus lifts a prayer of surrender, accepting the consequences of God's divine will *even though he does not want to accept it*. It takes three attempts to win the peace. Then Jesus is able to say to his disciples, "Behold the hour is at hand, and the Son of Man is betrayed into the hands of sinners." And, having submitted to his Father, Jesus moves toward triumphant fulfillment.

When Jesus prayed "Thy will be done," he submitted to God. He spoke the words deliberately and only after protracted agonizing. We, on the other hand, are not always in a state of surrender; moreover, we say the words perfunctorily and without first ascertaining God's will.

Let's look at some occasions when this prayer may be

appropriate. Interestingly, one occasion is when God's will is *not* clear to us. We find an example in the book of Acts. Paul plans to go to Jerusalem to proclaim the gospel. The prophet Agabus and the prophesying daughters of Philip warn him that great dangers await him there, but he persists in going.

"What are you doing, weeping and breaking my heart?" Paul cries to his would-be protectors. "For I am ready not only to be imprisoned, but even to die at Jerusalem for the name of the Lord Jesus." (Acts 21:13)

"And when he would not be persuaded," Luke records, "we ceased and said, 'The will of the Lord be done.' "

Paul's friends could see only danger where Paul saw victory, but because they sensed his dedication to the Lord, they could say, "The will of the Lord be done." They knew God could be trusted to take care of Paul.

We too can offer these words as an expression of trust when we are unable to discern God's intentions.

Chet Dawson accepted a call to a progressive church in a midwestern suburb. Within five years, membership tripled. People loved Chet's buoyant personality and compassionate nature. When he resigned to take another pastorate, the congregation pleaded with him to reconsider.

"You must be out of your mind. That decaying church you're taking will soon be a ghetto," sputtered one prominent layman.

"You have great potential, Chet. Please don't throw it away," another pleaded.

The church members implored, but to no avail. Then, in desperation—and yet in witness to their faith—they repeated the ancient words of Agabus: "Thy will be done, O Lord."

When we earnestly seek the mind of Christ (as the people sought his will for Chet) and we come out on different ends, what next? In this case, Chet remained steadfast in his conviction that God was calling him to the new pastorate. His loving congregation, on the other hand, said, "We do not understand, and we think you're making a mistake; nevertheless, we will put you in the hands of God and trust that his purpose will be accomplished." That's a constructive step.

There is another similar context for using this prayer. An example: After seven years of rapid advancement with one airline, Ted decided it was time for him to change companies. Two firms made attractive offers. Ted wanted to determine God's wish for him, but no answer came. Then he made a prayer of total commitment: "God, you show the way, for you know best." The following morning, one of the companies increased its offer. Believing God had led in this, Ted accepted.

Like Ted, we often find ourselves not knowing what God desires, and our indecision torments us. This is the time for absolute submission, trusting that God, in his wisdom, will eventually show the way.

Effective prayer, filled with strength and feeling, comes from the inner man. As we affirm "Thy will be done," we acknowledge that God will work all things together for our good (Romans 8:28). As we submit, we align ourselves with God's perfect will.

Suggestions for Study and Practice

1. When you find yourself saying "Thy will be done," ask, "Do I really mean it? Am I honestly committing myself and my request to God's will? Am I sincerely seeking the best way, or am I copping out?"

2. With a friend or in a sharing group, list several typical prayer concerns: then discuss the possibly dangerous implications of committing these to God with a request that "Thy will be done."

6

Praying through or through praying?

The words tumbled out pell-mell, the story of a young man's conversion.

"And—and I thought you'd especially want to know," he said, nervously wiping his glasses. "You were my Sunday school teacher and always talked about belonging to God, so I wanted to tell you it's happened."

"Nothing could make me happier!" Mrs. Garbie exclaimed, tears filling her dark eyes. "I have prayed for you since you were six years old. You were so alert and eager to hear the Bible stories. Each day in prayer, I claimed you for God."

I was that young man. Unaware of my elderly teacher's intercession, I had gone through life feeling no need for God. Then a day came when God made himself known to me, a young man far from home in military service. My life was changed.

Dear Mrs. Garbie had, to use her own words, "prayed through."

"I prayed every day until God assured me you were going to become a Christian, and then I thanked him every day for hearing my prayer."

She *prayed through* where most of us offer a few words and are *through praying*. We ask once, perhaps twice, and stop. "Why should I keep bugging God?"

Effective prayer means petitioning until something happens: Either the answer comes, or you pray in another direction, or you conclude, "This is just not his will."

Elijah shows us how to importune. Israel has suffered a three-year drought, and the prophet prays for rain. Nothing happens. He prays a second time—a third—a fourth. The seventh time, his servant reports "a little cloud like a man's hand is rising out of the sea." (I Kings 18:42–44) The prayer is answered, and even before Elijah can race down the mountain, rain drenches the countryside.

The Christian who wants to achieve effective communication with God must learn to persevere in prayer. Jesus teaches us that great lesson twice in Luke's gospel.

Chapter 18 begins, "And he told them a parable, to the effect that they ought always to pray and not lose heart." This is followed by the story of the widow who appeals to a wicked judge. The first time, he ignores her. Undaunted, she petitions a second time, and a third. Finally, to free himself from the constant irritation, the judge declares, "Though I neither fear God nor regard man, yet because this widow bothers me, I will vindicate her, or she will wear me out by her continual coming."

The parable concludes with Jesus' words, "And will not God vindicate his elect, who cry to him day and night?"

Perseverance!

In Luke 11, the disciples discover Jesus praying in a secluded place. "Teach us to pray. Teach us to pray like John (the Baptist) taught his disciples," they ask. They may want a set prayer such as religious leaders prescribed, or they may desire instructions on how to communicate with the Father.

Jesus responds by teaching them the Lord's Prayer. Within its few sentences, we discover three basic elements: worship, petition, and confession.

The prayer begins with worship—acknowledging God: "Our Father. . .Holy is your name. . . ." Recognition of God's rule over life leads us to petition: "Provide for our daily needs." Finally, realizing our dependence on God makes us see our own faithlessness and failure, so confession follows: "Forgive us, Lord. . .and as we experience forgiveness from you, we are enabled to forgive others."

Jesus gave this prayer as a model ("When you pray, say. . ."), and he continued his teaching by telling of a man who receives a late visitor. A conscientious host, he must provide refreshments, but alas, he has none. He runs to his neighbor's house and raps on the door.

"Jacob, lend me some bread. My friend has come to visit just now, and there is nothing in our house to eat."

"Go away. Can't you see the lights are out? We're all in bed. Come back in the morning."

"No, no, Jacob. Tonight Isaac is here. Please, just three loaves."

Jesus concludes, "I tell you, though he will not get up and give him anything because he is his friend, yet because of his importunity he will rise and give him whatever he needs." (Luke 11:8)

Jesus' parable stresses importunity in prayer. Then, beginning at verse nine, he gives an interpretation: "And I tell you, Ask, and it will be given you; seek. . .knock. . ."

The verbs *ask*, *seek*, *knock* are written in the Greek in the present tense, imperative mood. A clearer translation, and a perfectly legitimate one, makes them present continuous in the English: "Be asking. . .be seeking. . .be knocking." Or, put another way, "Ask and keep on asking, seek and keep on seeking, knock and then keep on knocking."

The lesson is that we must pray. . .and pray. . .and keep on praying. Our persistence reveals how seriously we pray. Scarcely anyone will continue to ask for something he doesn't desire deeply.

In a supermarket, five-year-old Brian "helped" his mother shop. Every attractive package became the object of battle: "Mommy, buy this one!"

At one point he yelled, "Mommy, get me this candy bar!"

"No, Brian, we have candy at home."

"But I want one now!"

"Not this time."

Brian, undaunted, repeated his request four times, each louder than before. The mother, embarrassed by condescending smiles as grocery carts passed, took Brian by the arm. "Listen here, young man, *no candy*!"

The brown eyes begged. "Please, just one, Mommy."

He got the candy bar. Importunity!

Imagine how it would be if everyone prayed and received instant delivery. "Give me *this* one, God." "Give me *that* one, please." No requirements, no second thoughts, no looking ahead at consequences. Just "Give me, please." Isn't God more than a genie called up to satisfy our whims?

Sometimes when we make a request, the answer arrives promptly. Other times we pray and wait, and nothing happens. Do we persist or stop?

Beacon Hill Church became stirred up for revival after their pastor preached a series of messages.

"We are going to pray every day for God to change lives!" cried the pastor.

"We shall pray faithfully until an awakening comes," asserted the Sunday school superintendent.

"We intend praying until a harvest of souls is brought into the kingdom!" boasted the lay leader.

Enthusiasm swept through the congregation. Within six months, however, the fervor had died and few prayers were being offered. Either the people lacked solid commitment in the first place, or they grew tired and doubtful. Lacking persistence, they failed.

Oftentimes we throw ourselves behind a cause and vow to pray in its behalf, but impatience, boredom, indifference, apathy—these and other sinister forces erode our iron will. To persist means continuing to pray in trust even when there is little or no evidence the request is being heard. It means praying through in spite of hindrances or discouragement.

Being forced to pray insistently makes us rethink; as a result, we sometimes withdraw or modify our request.

James wanted to be a success in the business world. "God,

make me successful so I can give more money to the church," he prayed. Although he asked regularly and intently, his financial situation didn't improve.

"One morning as I prayed this petition," he related, "an inner voice said, 'James, how can you pray that way? Since you don't tithe now out of $800 a month, will tithing from $1,200 be easier? You'd squander it and keep asking for more! Be faithful with what you have.' I learned my lesson and thanked God for what I did have!"

Waiting sometimes makes the answer more precious. When our son was nine, he wanted a bicycle. I was doing graduate work, and we didn't have much money. We saw no way to get John Mark a bicycle; yet, in our daily family worship, he prayed, "And God, help me get a bicycle."

Determined not to be the only boy in the neighborhood without wheels, John Mark saved thirty cents each week from his fifty-cent allowance. Then, at Christmas, friends sent an unexpected check. We bought the bicycle. The waiting made John Mark appreciate the bike even more.

God doesn't always answer immediately, but if we persist and if our request pleases God, the answer comes. The object is to pray—pray—and continue to pray.

What needs do you have? Are you praying through—or, are you through praying?

Suggestions for Study and Practice

1. Focus on a personal concern which can be resolved within the next few days (a decision to make, a person to talk to, a step in spiritual growth you can experience, etc.) Determine to "pray through." See how it goes.

2. Think of past prayers. Ask yourself, "Have I 'prayed through' as a regular practice? How personally involved have I been in intercessory prayer?"

3. What kinds of concerns have been worthy of persistent prayers in your own life? Has the need for continued petitioning screened out shallow concerns?

4. Share your experiences and insights with a friend or group.

7

To bless and to wrestle

In an authoritative voice, our six-year-old son said to the rest of the family, "Okay, are there any prayer requests?" He listened carefully to our list, and then he began to pray, "Lord, bless Uncle Carl; bless the Hollanders, who are missionaries; help the sore on my leg get well; help Daddy at work. . . ."

That sort of prayer may be appropriate for a six-year-old, but for a teen-ager or adult? I doubt it.

Do your prayers often employ the words "bless" and "help"? What do you mean when you say, "God bless Luther Jones"? Do you really care about Luther's problems? If not, are you genuinely engaging in *intercessory* prayer?

If your prayers for others are nothing more than saying "bless" and adding a name, why not streamline your efforts? Wouldn't it be more efficient to pray, "God, bless the following: Harold, Susan, Dr. Morgan. . ." This seems as ridiculous as a situation I observed at a midweek prayer service.

The pastor stood at the rostrum taking prayer requests.

"I have two," called an elderly woman.

"Thank you. Two for our Sister Ames," he said, jotting down her contribution.

"Put me down for four," volunteered a red-haired man in back.

"Four for Mr. Potter. Someone else?"

When all the numbers had been called out, the pastor totaled them. Then he prayed: "God in Heaven, we bring 37 requests to you tonight. Bless them, we pray in Jesus' name, Amen."

This "numbers game" we had prayed (or played) set me thinking: How many devices that we use and consider legitimate are actually gimmicks? Like prayer lists, for example. A list can be helpful, especially if each name represents a special need, either stated or felt, but to pray perfunctorily for the same names day after day can become a monotonous roll call. When I began using a list, I conscientiously remembered every name; otherwise, I would have felt guilty. Even so, my prayers weren't satisfying; I began to feel like a machine. "Is this the most effective way to pray?" I asked myself. I doubted it. Still, it was hard for me to break my old habits. Nowadays I occasionally lapse into using "mimeographed" prayers.

I was helped by reading prayers in the Bible, especially in the New Testament. When Jesus' disciples prayed, situations changed: People were healed or converted. Paul's prayers burned with zeal. Paul told several congregations that he prayed for them daily, and I'm sure it was more than including them on a list.

There's a significant commentary on intense prayer in Colossians 4:12. Paul says Epaphras is "always wrestling on your behalf in his prayers." (Weymouth Translation) This suggests deep personal involvement and self-sacrifice, in contrast to the chanting of names. True prayer requires giving ourselves to people. So, when we glibly toss in a "bless Walter," we should ask, "Have I really opened my heart to his need?"

What does "bless" mean? One dictionary says "to invoke

divine favor or to wish prosperity or success for another." Is the request answered if Walter inherits a fortune? Or finds a good wife? What do I mean if I say someone "blessed me out"? Modern usage has emptied the word "bless" of concrete meaning. We need to rethink the concept of blessing; at the same time, we need to be more specific in our application of the word. If Henry needs guidance in choosing a career, why not specify this need? The more specific the praying, the more involved I become.

Much has been said about the effects of prayer on the "prayee." We need also to think of how the "pray-er" is affected. By taking time to intercede on another's behalf, we are linked with that person in a mutual bond. The one who prays gains insight and understanding, which should result in true Christian fellowship.

Our church learned this almost by accident. After completing two years of college, Jenny was to go to the Dominican Republic for the summer to assist missionaries in distributing gospel literature. Because of prior obligations, we felt we could offer Jenny only a small honorarium. We were like Peter and John at the Gate Beautiful, where they encountered a cripple begging for alms. (Acts 3) "I have no silver and gold, but I give you what I have," Peter replied, whereupon the lame limbs leaped with new strength.

"Jenny, we want to share with you in your ministry," said several members as Jenny departed. "We will pray for you every day."

At this time, twelve of us were meeting weekly to find ways to deepen our prayer lives. Arnold, seventy years old, spoke up. "You know, we promised to pray for Jenny. I wonder how much good we're really doing." A discussion followed.

"I know what it's like in a strange land," said May, a former missionary. "Missionaries have special problems. Could we agree to pray specifically for some of those needs? Things like coping with a strange culture, the physical problems of living in the tropics, and maintaining good relationships with other missionaries."

For the next few minutes, we put ourselves in Jenny's

place, exploring the hardships she might be facing. Then each of us agreed to pray in Jenny's behalf regarding one of these problems.

When the church received its first letter from Jenny, we learned she had to make a half-hour climb each dawn to get to a mountaintop village where she tramped from house to house distributing gospels and tracts. At sunset, her party trudged back down the mountain.

Later, after Jenny had received a letter telling her how we were praying for her, she wrote:

> Every morning I dragged myself up the mountain. "How can I keep going?" I kept asking myself. At noon we stop to eat the sandwiches Eddie brings. Tuesday, Eddie brought mail from home, including your letter.
>
> It is wonderful to know a group of people pray daily for my needs. Going down the mountain that evening, I felt I could run all the way. All tiredness left my body.
>
> I do my work each day, coming home satisfied, feeling God has been with me. I know your prayers have made the difference. Maybe it was a psychological breakthrough after reading your letter, I don't know. But as far as I am concerned, it is a miracle of God's doing. God met me, and now I'm a more effective worker. Thanks to all of you.

God ministered to Jenny—*and to us*. Instead of tacking "bless" onto routine petitions, we had given of ourselves. In company with Epaphras, we experienced what it means to wrestle in prayer on another's behalf.

Suggestions for Study and Practice

1. When you're tempted to use "bless" routinely in a prayer, ask yourself, "What do I really mean?" Translate your intentions into more specific language.

2. If "bless" keeps popping up in your thoughts as you pray, ask yourself why. Have you fallen into the lazy habit of letting your mind "idle" while you pray? You may wish to explore prayer habits with others.

3. List other words and phrases that are so overworked as to have become trite. Is the lack of meaning inherent in the words themselves, or in our use of them?

4. Your group might, as an amusing project, write a prayer replete with "bless"-type language, then translate it into more effective words.

8

Reminded by sirens, watches, and coins

"My problem is, I don't often think about God," Eve said in our sharing group. "At church or with this group, God is real—I can pray and I have the feeling he hears. But when I'm doing housework, taking care of the children, or shopping, I'm simply not conscious of God. Oh, if a problem arises, I pray, but because things usually go along rather evenly, God seldom enters my thoughts."

Eve's candid admission encouraged each of us, in turn, to acknowledge that we failed to think about God in our daily activities.

"We should decide to pray more every day," Ron suggested.

"That's not the answer," Bertha spoke up. "When Nixon was elected president, I resolved to pray for him every day. A year later, the fact hit me that he had not been in my prayers half a dozen times. Resolutions aren't enough."

"We forget too easily," remarked Ron. "We're caught up in our private worlds and personal problems. For example,

God just doesn't seem to break into my job."

I acknowledged that I, too, had problems with prayer. This shocked many of the group.

"Being an ordained minister, your business is 'God-business,' " Ron commented.

"You're always talking about Christ as you preach, teach, and counsel. You're lucky not to be out in the secular world the way the rest of us are."

"The fact is," I confessed, "in my *busyness*, I forget God *the person* even while I'm engaged in his *business*. My problems are no different from yours."

The discussion continued. If God is to be the center of our lives, we reasoned, he must be given allegiance in the workaday world as well as in the church. But how? Each of us agreed to search for answers.

For me, the answer came on a Friday evening, the first night in months that Shirley and I were able to be home alone. Our two teen-aged daughters were on dates, with special permission to stay out late, and our son was spending the night with a friend. It promised to be a delightful evening. As we ate supper, Shirley said she was going to prop herself on pillows and read a book. I planned to tackle a stack of magazines and journals. Later we would make popcorn and watch TV without doing battle with the youngsters over which channel to watch.

The telephone interrupted our supper tete-a-tete. No, my son was not in. Ten minutes later: No, Daughter Number One wasn't home. Yes, I'd take a message.

The pattern was set. No popcorn was popped; Shirley's reading advanced only five pages; I scanned one magazine. Even the TV programs were rendered incoherent by interruptive ringing. By eight o'clock we'd lost count of the calls—none intended for Shirley or me. Our illusion of solitude vanished and so did my cheery telephone voice.

"Not again," I muttered to Shirley as I grabbed the tormenting instrument another time. "I feel like tearing out this menace to civilization."

"HELLO!" I challenged the invisible intruder.

Click.

"The nerve! Hanging up on me!"

"You probably frightened him to death," said Shirley.

Almost immediately, the phone rang again. As I touched the receiver, a prayer sprang to my lips: "Lord, speak through me as I answer."

In that instant, a revelation burst upon me, a revelation which I shared with the group the following Wednesday.

"This much the Lord taught me," I concluded. "Even the telephone can be a reminder to pray. Now, every time the phone rings, I offer the prayer, 'Lord, speak through me.' "

My testimony started others thinking. We agreed to look for additional reminders to turn ourselves toward God during our daily activities.

When we met again, Doris said, 'I've been praying every time I hear a siren or see a police car. Is that the sort of thing you mean?" It was.

Now when Bob looks at his watch, he reminds himself, "My time is in your hands, O Lord."

Pete, formerly an impatient driver, turns his thoughts toward God while waiting at traffic lights.

Marty, a businessman, keeps a fifty-cent piece in a trouser pocket. Whenever he feels the coin, he thinks of the words from the hymn, "All that we have is thine alone, a gift, O Lord, from thee."

Bonnie, who works for an airline, began a new way of dealing with rude customers. "I look him in the eye and silently pray, 'Lord Jesus, fill me with love and understanding.' It really works, although I don't know whether it's the customer or me that God changes. Often the customer ends up smiling or even apologizing. That never happened to me before."

Find your own new ways to remind yourself to pray. "Draw near to God and he will draw near to you." (James 4:8)

Suggestions for Study and Practice

1. Ask yourself, "Why do I have trouble thinking about God during my daily affairs?" You may wish to jot down the reasons.

2. Choose *one* prayer reminder (either a method mentioned in this chapter or one of your own) and use it several days.

3. Does the use of a reminder condition you to be more aware of God's presence? Do you think you'll soon be able to "wean" yourself from this device and continue to think of God?

4. With a friend or group, talk about your successes and failures with prayer reminders.

9

Let God take care of himself

My wife, our three children, and I spent the day together. A picnic lunch, an hour's hike, and a few games, followed by a restful evening watching a circus special on TV.

Not an extraordinary day, yet a very good day. Why? Thinking back, I concluded that we'd enjoyed excellent relationships. We had mutual fellowship, love, and concern.

And that's how I see prayer: It's essentially a family relationship between God and his children. The essence of prayer must remain an exchange of love.

We must not assume that God always answers our requests, for this reduces prayer to asking and receiving. Petition is an element of prayer, but not the major one. Read the letters of Paul and discover that while petition is included in his prayers, it never becomes the totality. We petition because we recognize God as the doer and the source of power. First and foremost, however, prayer is communion.

When I was converted and first knew the experience of

talking to God, I asked for help. I prayed, "God have mercy on me. . .guide my life. . .give me strength for today's burdens." But now, as I grow in my relationship to Jesus Christ, my focus turns more and more toward fellowship. My motivation isn't entirely selfish, either, for this relationship enables me to make requests in behalf of others.

The query "Does God always answer prayer?" may stem from doubt, because true prayer proceeds from a relationship of trust and dependency. If I ask such a question, I need to inspect my motives. Why is this question important? Unasked may be other questions: "How can I convince myself that God always answers when I pray?" and "If I pray and don't get what I ask for, how can I justify God's silence?"

Because I believe God delights in assisting his people, I ask freely and without hesitation. If my request is specific, I know I will get a specific answer; God either grants my request or denies it. Simple?

No, life isn't always that simple. At one stage of growth, I wanted to believe that every specific request resulted in an equally specific, positive response. I now confess that I sometimes juggled the request around in my mind to make the answer come out right. Now I know that part of the difficulty was my doubt. I was not willing to let God take care of himself.

A godly woman was dying of cancer, and a group of us kept a prayer vigil, pleading for God to spare her life. She died. Most of us accepted her death. We had prayed and God had declined. But some were not satisfied, and two men even claimed victory. "God healed her of the *cancer*," they said. "What killed her was a *heart attack*." Is this spiritual honesty?

As I continue to walk with God, my compulsion to "prove him" becomes less vital. God can fend for himself—and I don't say that flippantly. To trust in Jesus Christ, I need not prove his ability to hear, nor do I need to scrutinize his answers. I accept God, and I accept life as being under his control. In my heart, I know I can never prove God or God's working in our lives to anyone who does not wish to believe.

Five of us were traveling across the Serengeti Plain of Africa. The rains had set in, and our four-wheel-drive vehicle became impossibly imbedded in heavy mud. The area, on the edge of a wild game preserve, had been vacated in a government resettlement program, so the chance that someone would come along was remote. Fearing we might be stranded for days or even weeks, we prayed for God's help.

Within an hour, a group of hunters appeared. They were returning to their village, and they stopped to help us. We called their intervention an answer to prayer.

A critic could cry, "Coincidence! The men would have come by, prayer or no prayer." Perhaps, but to us, it didn't matter. We were in need, we prayed, help came—and that was sufficient for us. What would I gain by arguing?

Behind our desires to prove God's actions to skeptics, we may discover flaws in our own belief. The more uncertain a man is of his worth, the harder he works to prove his value. The exhibitionist male may be seeking affirmation of his masculinity. The promiscuous girl may be seeking assurance of her attractiveness. The louder we pound the desk, the higher we pitch our voices in defense of the faith, the more uncertain we prove ourselves to be. Once, as I argued a doctrinal issue with a colleague, he responded, "Wait. Speak a little louder there. Your argument is growing weak." Perhaps this explains why we so loudly and insistently assert, "God always answers prayer!" We're trying to convince ourselves!

"I know God answers prayer," Harold testified. "We wanted to move, and we asked the Lord to help us sell our house. It sold within two weeks." Harold is saying that the sale proves God answers prayer. (It's also possible to hear this as a boast of his prowess at prayer.)

How much better to speak of God's involvement in our lives in the context of our faith in his love and power. We strive to prove God's power, but he hasn't asked us to do this. Our quiet, unassuming witness may be more effective than our verbal advocacy. God can fend for himself.

Not being able to prove God scientifically or verify him mathematically should not arouse our consternation; rather, it should strengthen our peace.

God can take care of himself. *Our* task is to love and serve him. God hears us because of our relationship of love.

Suggestions for Study and Practice

1. Let your prayer time center on enriching your fellowship with God. Do your conversations with God strengthen your personal relationship with the Father? If so, does this fellowship make it seem less important to prove God to yourself and to others?

2. Why do you attempt to justify God? Is there a biblical basis, or does the compulsion spring out of your own mind?

3. The next time you're tempted to try to prove God by reciting material benefits, try instead to speak of what trust in God means in your life.

4. Try this exercise within your group. Have one member take the role of a person attempting to prove God's power by citing an answer to prayer, while another member acts as a devil's advocate and attempts to disprove the spiritual nature of the event. Remember, serious insights can come out of our lighter experiences, so don't mind a little humor. Does this role-playing demonstrate the ineffectiveness of trying to prove God?

10

To pray and praise in public

Jimmy Andrews, a newly elected deacon, prayed the "blessing" at our church family night supper, which was attended by about eighty people, including quite a few youngsters.

Jimmy intoned, "Upon this food, O Jesus, thou Son of God, the Living Christ, the One omniscient, omnipotent, omnipresent, imminent, yet transcendent, the ultimate reality, thou art the perfectly unique, divine emanation, the partaker of a single substance, united organically and indissolubly with the Eternal First Cause. . ."

A freckled-faced lad was moved to nudge his neighbor and ask, "Jesus *who*?"

In public prayer, it's terribly easy to pile on superlatives until, finally, meaning collapses.

All of us "get caught" at one time or another and are asked to pray. I don't know anyone who says he enjoys praying in public. Why are people reluctant (even afraid) to lead in prayer? Perhaps it's because prayer is intensely personal. When we converse with God, we open our innermost lives (if we are honest).

Our uneasiness is heightened by our feeling that those present (usually we're more conscious of our fellow human listeners than our divine hearer) are hanging onto every word—even analyzing our thoughts and tearing them apart. But think back to the last public prayer you heard. How much do you recall? The general theme? Even less?

We also have trouble because we lack experience. We don't know how to begin or end. Often our discomfort shows in superfluous words and rambling thoughts. Fearing we will forget something, we include everything. A member of a Sunday school class was called upon to pray. Obviously caught unawares, the young lady prayed. . .and prayed. . . and prayed, finally concluding with: "And, Lord, if I've forgotten anyone, bless them anyway. Amen."

The use of archaic language sometimes reduces the meaningfulness of public prayer. Elizabethan forms were easily understood in Elizabethan times, but few of us think in these terms today. Yet, we fear we'll profane the Almighty by addressing him in the vernacular, and so we add outdated "polite" suffixes—"Oh, God, Thou knowest. . .Thou shouldest. . ." Small wonder our tongues and thoughts get twisted.

Lengthy, repetitious, and contrived prayers hold little meaning for either the speaker or the congregation (and, I might add, for God). A few rules have helped me immensely.

Be brief. Contrast two prayers made during a convention. In the first instance, a minister was asked to offer the introduction. We stood for twenty-three minutes (I have a longstanding habit of timing everything). When he concluded, a sigh swept through the auditorium. A lady standing near me remarked, "He must have been saving his private devotions for a week."

The next evening as we awaited the blessing, we steeled ourselves for another "geographical" prayer (i.e., "around the world in fifteen minutes"). Instead, the person prayed:

"Father, for this food we thank you. Amen."

He sat down and began eating. Confusion showed on many faces, but the lesson got through. No more rambling prayers during that convention.

Prayers for missionary needs, war orphans, campus unrest—all have a time and place, but ask, "Is this the time and place?"

Be specific. If you deliver the opening prayer, make it an opening prayer and not a sermon. Pray specifically, and when you're through, sit down. When asked to pray, Clarence demonstrated he had been faithful in his devotional study. He told us about it, interpreted it, enlarged upon it, and then exhorted us. We learned not to call on him often.

Pray honestly. When beautiful phrases get in the way of the content, are we really praying honestly? One of the most honest and delightful prayers I've heard came after the leader of a prayer meeting requested, "Will someone please open in prayer?" After a pained silence, Buck began, "Well, God, I guess I've got the longest tongue in the bunch and I'm getting nervous with no one saying anything, so here goes. . ."

Pray directly to God. In offering public prayer, we address the Lord, not people. Choose the form of address with which you feel most comfortable. If it is easier for you to pray in the traditional "thee" and "thou" form, by all means continue, but don't feel bound to do so.

Remember, too, that you are not giving God the news of the day, or informing him of any secrets; instead, you are offering praise, confession, and petition on behalf of yourself and the listeners. In a "faith-type" Bible training center in England, the student body held protracted prayer. One earnest student concluded his oral petition, "And, Lord, thou knowest I need shoes, for mine are nearly worn out and have holes in them, and, Father, thou knowest I wear size ten." To whom was the student praying?

Pray corporately. In public prayer, one individual audibly expresses the needs and feelings of the many. Except when personal concerns are solicited, public prayers are supposed to represent the general praises and petitions of the congregation.

The listener also participates. The next time you are in the company of believers and public prayer is offered, pray with the petitioner. As he expresses your praises, your desires, your problems, acknowledge and affirm them.

Public prayer needn't be a burden. It can be a meaningful expression of a united group of believers in Jesus Christ.

Suggestions for Study and Practice

1. This week, in your public prayers, including grace at the family table, try to be brief, specific, and honest.

2. As you hear public prayer, listen attentively and make it *your* prayer.

3. Ask yourself, "How can I be more at ease in praying before others?" In your group, discuss ways to overcome uneasiness or fear.

4. Take turns praying aloud together in your family and/or sharing group. (Allow anyone who does not wish to pray aloud to remain silent.) Is it easier to pray aloud within a group you know intimately than in public? If so, what does this suggest to you about bringing our congregations into closer fellowship?

11

Problems with the promises

Six of us sat around the conference table in Doran's office. That morning, as every Wednesday, we were sharing spiritual experiences. Doran read verse 10 of Psalm 91, "No evil shall befall you, no scourge come near your tent."

"Hallelujah!" Bill broke in. "Isn't that promise wonderful —no plague or disaster coming near us."

"But what happens if trouble does strike a Christian family?" I challenged. "What if you or your wife come down with some dread disease? Does that mean God has failed to keep his promises?"

Dave asserted that "the Bible contains more than 30,000 promises for believers. These promises are ours. Always."

In faith I cried out, "Amen!" But deep within me, I knew that my experiences did not match those promises. I've had a lot of hard situations. In the mission field, a band of men beat me severely because I preached the gospel. Another time my wife lay in a hospital after a traffic accident, not expected to live. On several other occasions, we didn't have food and didn't know where the next meal would come from. Why didn't the promises of immunity from evil spare us those situations?

It becomes increasingly clear to me that God does not always provide special protection for his people. To ask for and expect deliverance out of every tribulation says we don't grasp the intent of the Christian life. God doesn't promise to take us out of troubles—only to see us through them.

Paul experienced imprisonment, beatings, stonings, shipwreck, dangers from robbers and enemies, and hunger. (2 Corinthians 11:23–28) Suppose someone had quoted Psalm 37:25: "I have been young, and now am old; yet I have not seen the righteous forsaken or his children begging bread." This verse, taken alone, would suggest Paul lacked righteousness; otherwise, he wouldn't have had so many ills to befall him.

Hebrews 11:37–38 lists those martyrs for the faith who suffered mocking and scourging, chains and imprisonment. They were stoned, sawn in two, killed with the sword. They went about in skins of sheep and goats, destitute, afflicted, ill treated; they wandered over deserts and mountains and lived in caves. Yet men and women of faith and courage continued to profess Christ in the face of pain and persecution.

"Can we expect never to experience hardships?" I asked of a friend. Instantly becoming a defender of the faith and protector of my spirit, he took exception to my implied statement. "But the Bible promises rewards for Christian living—and, well, it's God's word. You can't deny the scriptures, can you?"

"No, I'm a believer in the scriptures. I find no fault with the Bible, or with the promises."

Then how do I reconcile the seeming gap between life and the Bible?

Let me pose a few preliminary questions: If there are indeed 30,000 promises in the Bible, how do we know which ones we can claim *in any given situation*? Is the Bible a "grab bag" of promises? Does God hold out the book like a box of assorted chocolates and say, "Pick what you want"? I certainly hope you don't have this concept. On the other hand, God does impress promises upon us in specific situations.

Tom was overburdened. He was paying for a home and providing for his wife and three young daughters. When he bought the house, Mattie was working, but now an illness had incapacitated her. Tom prayed for help but received no consolation. Desperate, one day he opened his Bible and read:

> Fear not, for I have redeemed you; I have called you by name, you are mine. When you pass through the waters I will be with you; and through the rivers, they shall not overwhelm you; when you walk through fire you shall not be burned, and the flame shall not consume you.
> (Isaiah 43:1–2)

"God spoke to me through this scripture and told me he was with me," Tom said. He soon got eight hours a week of overtime, and, a bit later, Mattie was able to return to work.

The promise brought peace to Tom. Suppose, however, he had selected the verse, "Take delight in the Lord, and he will give you the desires of your heart." (Psalm 37:4) He could have said, "God, I'm delighting in you, so take care of my monthly payments." Would he have received a check in the mail? God spoke words appropriate to Tom's needs—he promised Tom the strength of his presence. With this assurance, Tom was able to work through his financial problems.

As we hear God speak to us through the Bible, we need to keep the promises in perspective, remembering two things.

First, there are no automatic results. The promises do not exist for random use; rather, God makes them a reality for us in a specific situation. A verse, a phrase, or a promise takes on meaning *at the right moment.*

After that gang of robbers broke into our house in Africa, the district officer urged me to obtain a gun permit. "You never know when thieves will come this way again," he said. "Your mission station is isolated, and you have no protection."

I conferred with another missionary who had already taken out a permit. He reminded me that in the days of Queen

Esther, the Jews were a target for the Persians and prepared themselves for battle.

His rationale seemed logical; however, wanting to be certain, I prayed. Another Old Testament story came to mind. The king of Persia agreed to let Ezra return to Palestine and offered him an escort. Ezra refused, explaining, "For I was ashamed to ask the king for a band of soldiers and horsemen to protect us against the enemy on our way; since we had told the king, 'The hand of our God is for good upon all that seek him, and the power of his wrath is against all that forsake him.' So we fasted and besought our God for this, and he listened to our entreaty." (Ezra 8:22–23)

This was my answer. I didn't apply for a gun permit, and robbers never troubled us again. We often said, "The Lord is our protection."

Second, scripture speaks to us only when energized by the Holy Spirit. Of itself, the Bible is only words on a page. Before we can appropriate the living Word of God, there must be an intervention of the Holy Spirit. Have you read scripture and found it devoid of meaning? Yet, on another occasion, you felt, "This is God speaking to me."

The Holy Spirit makes the biblical writings come alive. Years ago I learned a beautiful little chorus:

Every promise in the book is mine,
Every chapter, every verse, every line.
All are tokens of his love divine.
Every promise in the book is mine.

But they are mine—in the sense of appropriation—only when the Holy Spirit makes them a reality for me.

If my son is burning up with a fever of 106 degrees, it seems futile to say, "God, your word declares no plague will come near me." The plague has already come. What I need is help in my helplessness. The Holy Spirit may make alive the verse, ". . .for I am the Lord, your healer." (Exodus 15:26) Or, "The Lord gave, and the Lord has taken away." (Job 1:21) Or, he may give no promise at all.

Why do we pull back from acknowledging the infinite dimensions of God's wisdom and power? *God is the Lord!* Who are we to shake our fist and cry out, "God, you promised no plagues! Explain yourself!"

Carelessly chosen scripture holds little meaning, but when the Holy Spirit makes a promise come alive, something within responds, "Yes, Lord." Then we have assurance.

Jesus underwent forty days of temptation in the wilderness. Both Luke and Matthew record three of the temptations, including the devil's quoting (of all things) a promise from Psalm 91.

> "If you are the Son of God, throw yourself down; for it is written, 'He will give his angels charge of you,' and 'On their hands they will bear you up, lest you strike your foot against a stone.' " (Matthew 4:6)

Suppose Jesus had acted on the basis of the promise which Satan quoted and had thrown himself off the pinnacle of the temple. What would have happened? I suggest he would have fallen to his death!

God had, at an earlier time, made the safeguarding promise, but the Spirit had not "energized" it in that situation. The devil used this scripture as a taunt. Yet, that same verse can come alive. It did for me.

I wanted to visit a troubled area where the tribal leaders resented missionaries coming in and teaching the people to turn from the worship of a mountain. Our African evangelists had persisted in the face of fierce opposition. I was warned that some of the people had threatened to kill me if I showed up. I felt afraid, and I prayed: "Lord, show me if it's your will for me to go, and I'll go knowing you'll either take care of me or give me the grace to die faithfully." A verse came to mind. "For he will give his angels charge of you to guard you in all your ways." (Psalm 91:11)

I went. We had a splendid meeting, and no one threatened me. The Holy Spirit had spoken, making the promise mine *for that situation*. Another time it might have been inappropriate and ineffectual.

Perhaps I've made guidance and assurance sound difficult. It need not be. When the Holy Spirit speaks, we can then sing, "*This* promise in the book is mine."

Suggestions for Study and Practice

1. How do we know when a promise is ours for a given situation? Share with your group any experiences you may have had.

2. What dangers can you see in claiming "Every promise in the book is mine"?

3. I've suggested that the Bible's promises become energized by the Holy Spirit. Can sharing groups be helpful in providing a setting? Exchange ideas with other persons.

12

Even our enemies

The Reverend Harold Weston was a dud. His preaching was dreary; his voice grated on our nerves; his grammar embarrassed us. He had two facial expressions: mouth open and mouth closed. Besides, I didn't like the man. I went to him once with a serious problem. Mr. Weston listened, gave me good advice—and told his wife. She told everyone! Further, he resented my college degree. Once he remarked, "Cec thinks he owns the world because he's got a little education, doesn't he?"

I attended services under his ministry for a year; yet I remember praying for Mr. Weston only twice. Both prayers went something like, "Lord, get that man out of our church before he completely kills it!"

I look back in shame. I judged without love, criticized without caring, and rejected without compassion. I found it easier to publicize his foibles and failures than to pray for him and our relationship.

I wish I had been more like Samuel. In I Samuel there appears a remarkable story. Samuel had been the God-appointed leader and unquestioned prophet of Israel. Then, one day, the people rejected him:

"Samuel, we recognize your work. You have been a good man, but we don't want you anymore. We insist on a king."

The prophet faced the people and replied, "You err! You are going astray, rejecting the divine plan and the Divine One."

"We don't care! We're tired of the way things are going. Raise up a king to rule over us!"

Samuel pleaded with them, "You must be made aware of what you're doing. You're rejecting God!"

They refused to yield.

Samuel didn't slink away or shake his fist or whine over his ruined career. Instead, he called out, "God will provide a king, acquiescing to your demands." And he added, "Far be it from me that I should sin against the Lord by ceasing to pray for you."

Samuel knew God's way: a way of love in the midst of rejection, care in a time of contempt, and compassion in a moment of contention. He prayed for those who despised him.

It is right to pray for others—not only friends and relatives, but also those who dislike us or whom we dislike. Prayer is an obligation of God's people; it is basic to the Christian life. Yet, prayer surpasses duty. We pray because we love. What better way of expressing concern than talking to the Father in someone's behalf? Prayer provides the entrance to involvement. Even as we pray, we remember Jesus' words, "Without me you can do nothing." We ask; he works.

Prayer becomes an expression of attitude, a measuring stick of concern. If we have no interest, no compassion, then obviously we do not *really* pray.

If it is right that we pray for others, is it not a sin when we refuse to pray? Samuel said, "God forbid that I should sin by not praying for you." When we fail to pray for others, we turn our backs on them and also on God, his commands, and our relationship to him. In effect, we deny his existence as the God of all comfort.

"That woman!" my friend said. "She's a mean, gossip-carrying old crow. She picks up everything she hears, exaggerates it, and then passes it on to everyone who will listen. She's the cause of most of the trouble in our church."

"Have you ever prayed for her?" I asked.

She turned and gazed out the window. "She's hurt me so many times that I just can't find it in my heart to pray for her. Besides, it wouldn't do any good. She'll never change."

I know the feeling: I've lived there myself. I didn't think God could ever change the Reverend Mr. Weston, so I never asked him to try.

The commandment which troubles me more than any other is, "And thou shalt love thy neighbor as thyself." It convicts and condemns me, yet redemption is available. Prayer can express my love, enhance my concern.

Jesus, the great example, prayed for his crucifiers. Stephen, as his enemies hurled stones at his body, pleaded, "Lord, do not hold this sin against them." (Acts 7:60) Yet I, when someone says an ugly word about me, find it difficult to ask God's blessings for him.

From the beginning, Doyle disliked me. This didn't upset my spiritual balance, since he was only one person in the congregation (although he did hold a position of leadership). Over the months, however, I felt the effects of Doyle's opposition. Reports began drifting in: "Do you know what Doyle said? . . ."

I seethed in anger, then decided to pray for my nemesis. At least twice a day, I talked to the Lord about this man: "Lord, requite him for his sins." That's a scriptural prayer, for the Old Testament cries out, "Touch not mine anointed and do my prophets no harm." Imagine Doyle working against me—one who is trying to serve the Lord! I wasn't about to ask a divine blessing for my enemy—not when he deserved chastisement.

During this period of conflict, I agreed to join a sharing group across town. Imagine my surprise when I looked around the circle and saw Doyle. The man who had invited me had also invited him.

The leader divided us into small groups, and somehow Doyle and I formed two-thirds of a triad. We were asked to be as open as possible, and Doyle promptly fulfilled this request:

"I don't like you, Murphey. I think you're stuffy, snobbish, and cold. When you come into a room, you act like you own it and everyone in it."

He hesitated, and I steeled myself for another blast. Instead, he said: "But that doesn't absolve me, does it? I've let you down, working against you. This week I began praying for you, asking God to perfect you and use you to the utmost."

Doyle got through to me. We remain opposites in temperament and outlook; yet, we respect each other. I pray regularly for Doyle (he still irritates me!), and he talks to Jesus about me. We've both done some growing.

Now I can face some inner questions. Why did it trouble me to pray for Doyle? The answer: I didn't like him and didn't wish to see him blessed. I wanted my opinion of him confirmed in the eyes of the people. The thought has since flashed in my mind (the Holy Spirit at work?), "What would have happened if Doyle had changed radically into my idea of a Christian? What if Mr. Weston had brought revival in our church? Would I have been pleased?" Six months ago, the only honest answer would have been, "No!" Today I can say, "Yes, praise God."

That's what happens when we pray for our enemies. God may change them—and us. Are we prepared to accept radical answers to our prayers?

Suggestions for Study and Practice

1. Think of one person you don't like. Pray for that individual. What difficulties do you experience as you attempt to pray in his behalf?

2. Pray for an enemy over a period of time. Does the praying become easier? Does the prayer campaign move you toward any action?

3. Ask yourself these two questions:
   (a) Why do I have trouble forgiving my enemies and praying for their good?
   (b) What can I do to correct my attitude?

13

Nobody's perfect

Yesterday I confessed a sin. A little sin, but still a sin.

Bob's remark cut me. We were in a group, so I had no chance to retaliate (for which I later could give thanks to God). What right did he have to say that—and in front of other people! All that day the hurt and resentment lingered.

Then I talked to God and confessed, and I felt good. In I John 1:9, we read: "If we confess our sins, he is faithful and just, and will forgive our sins and cleanse us from all unrighteousness." When we fail to confess, we carry the weight of our guilt around with us, and it grows. Irritation becomes anger—anger becomes hostility—hostility turns into hatred.

David knew about hiding his guilt. "When I declared not my sin, my body wasted away through my groaning all day long. For day and night thy hand was heavy upon me; my strength was dried up as by the heat of summer." (Psalm 32:3–4)

When he confessed, things changed. "I said, I will confess my transgressions to the Lord, then thou didst forgive the guilt of my sin."

Everyone sins. We all fail God, let people down, live below our convictions. Guilt arises; we attempt to ignore it, but it haunts us. If, on the other hand, we're truly open to God, we confess our failure and accept the gift of forgiving love.

It's not easy for me to admit I'm wrong. I need to be right, to be justified. But when the Holy Spirit comes through, I can admit my failures.

One man expressed it like this—"I knew something had gone wrong between the Lord and me. It was as though I stood on one bank of the river and he on the other, and I couldn't find a bridge to get across." Isaiah said, ". . .your iniquities have made a separation between you and your God." (Isaiah 59:2)

Before real confession can come into our lives, we must be prompted by the Holy Spirit. "He will convict the world of sin," Jesus said. When the Holy Spirit works through our conscience, emotions, and attitudes, we feel contrite. This conviction moves us to bring our failure to God's attention in prayer.

The act of praying does not, in itself, afford relief. We may, for example, pray out of self-justification: "God, I'm sorry I lost my temper, but if Bob hadn't lipped off first. . ." Bob has his own problem to settle, but right now God deals with Cec Murphey!

Or, we can confess in vague terms. "God, forgive our many sins." In public prayer, this may be appropriate, but in private prayer, "our many sins" says little. Few of us have a problem praying, "Forgive us for not being concerned about the hungry people of the world." But what about, "God, there are people within two miles of our church who don't have enough food, and I don't do anything about it or feel any kind of concern"?

Many congregations regularly confess: "We have offended against thy holy laws. We have left undone those things which we ought to have done; and we have done those things which we ought not to have done." That scattergun prayer *can* be a deterrent to true confession.

"If we confess our sins, he is faithful and just. . . ," we recite; but does this really get to *our* sins? We've entered the right door, but stopped too soon.

There are three steps in real confession.

First: Starting with the general confession, I pray, "Forgive my lack of concern for people."

Second: I state specific actions (or lack of action). "God, forgive me for my lack of concern about Bob. I criticize him and don't love him as I ought." Now I've reached the specific act which troubles me. But I mustn't stop here.

Third: I go to the principle involved; otherwise, I can linger on the symptom and never get to the underlying cause. I ask, "Why don't I love Bob?" The reason may be obvious, or it may require searching.

"Lord, he's rude and loud and never listens." That's backwards—seeking justification for my sins. I have to keep probing. The principle is that I did not love Bob, my neighbor, as I love myself. True, he hurt my pride and bruised my ego. But again the principle: If I loved Bob in a truly Christian manner, his remarks would not *continue* to trouble me.

When I called Martin's office, he wasn't in and I left a message. The next day he hadn't answered and I called again. "Sorry, he's not in now but should return soon." By the time of my third call, I found myself feeling offended, but I reminded myself: "Martin's my friend. Perhaps he didn't get the messages, or has been too busy to reply. Isn't our friendship strong enough for me to overlook this?" I later discovered that a new secretary had failed to give him the messages.

Love for a person can forgive failures. Love says, "He's human like me."

There we have the three steps in confession: Begin with the general, go to the specific, then discover and expose the underlying principle. Now our act of confession is complete.

We need to remind ourselves that confession is *our* part of the action. Then we turn to God's part: "He is faithful. . .to forgive our sins and cleanse us from all unrighteousness." When genuine confession is made, forgiveness occurs. God declares us clean and pure again.

When guilt haunts us, what can we do?

Ron, now nearing forty, visited my office and said, "In college there was a class I had to pass or I'd not get my degree. A friend wrote my final exam paper and I got through. That sin has troubled me ever since."

"Have you ever confessed it to God?"

"Every night."

"Then you'd better stop."

"Why?" he asked incredulously.

"Either God lies when he promises forgiveness—or you're already forgiven. In either case, you don't need to keep talking about it."

"But I'm still troubled! What can I do?"

"Every time your mind centers on that event, consciously say to yourself, 'God forgave that.' You may have to say it a thousand times before you believe it, but once you believe it, you'll no longer be troubled."

Less than a week later, Ron dropped by my office. "Hey," he said, smiling, "I've been forgiven." And I smiled in return.

Suggestions for Study and Practice

1. Have you ever been conscious of the Holy Spirit bringing you to the point of confessing a sin?

2. In your private prayers, when you confess to God, go through the three steps: (1) general confession to (2) specific confession to (3) dealing with the principle involved. Why is step three important?

3. Questions to ponder: Must I confess each known sin and failure to God? Does he forgive me even when I don't confess? What difference does confession make?

14

"In Jesus' name"–a sort of magic?

Janet met God that morning. I was sitting almost directly behind her and saw it happen. When the pastor called the congregation to stand for prayer, Janet was caught with her left shoe off. She wiggled her foot, feeling for the shoe. As she stood, she clutched her right side (because of a slight gas pain, she told me later). I observed her body tense, then saw her smile. In that moment and in that position, God became a reality to Janet.

She told me later, "God spoke. I needed guidance, and he showed me what to do."

After that, when Janet intended to pray with earnestness, she took off her left shoe and stood clutching her right side. Upon assuming this stance, she expected God to speak.

Foolish superstition? Perhaps—but most of us have our prayer rituals. For example, we start a certain way ("Dear Heavenly Father" or "Lord, our God"), and some of us must *always, always* close with "in Jesus' name we pray."

A friend said to me, "I would no more drop 'in Jesus' name, amen' than I would stop reading a book before the last page. It belongs!"

But does it belong? Is my friend using magic words comparable to "abra cadabra" or "open sesame"? Is he, in effect, taking off his shoe and clutching his side, expecting instant success?

The issue isn't over the words themselves, but over the implications. Do we understand what we are saying when we pray "in Jesus' name"?

After all, Jesus said we should pray in his name:

"Whatever you ask in my name, I will do it." (John 14:13)

"If you ask anything in my name, I will do it." (John 14:14)

"Whatever you ask the Father in my name, he may give it to you." (John 15:16)

"If you ask anything of the Father, he will give it to you in my name." (John 16:23)

"Hitherto you have asked nothing in my name; ask, and you will receive." (John 16:24)

"In that day you will ask in my name." (John 16:26)

Here, six times in one section of John's gospel, the Lord exhorts disciples to ask in his name. What does it mean?

"The name of the Lord" appears throughout the Old Testament. It becomes synonymous with God himself.

In the ancient East, a name expressed a person's nature or character. This was true in some early Old Testament names. Adam means "man"; Esau means "red," which is how he looked at birth. Moses was "one pulled from the waters." Joshua delivered the people, and his name means "Yahweh is Savior."

For the ancients, to know the name of a deity meant to have power over him. While Jacob wrestled with a heavenly being, he asked, "What is your name?" He didn't ask out of idle curiosity; he believed that if he could trick this being into revealing his name, he could control him. The messenger, however, gave no answer.

God appeared to Moses in the burning bush, commanding him to go to Pharaoh. "Whom shall I say has sent me?"

Moses asked. "I am that I am (the living one)" came the answer. Not a name, but a revelation of God.

Praying "in the name of Jesus" says four things:

First, when Jesus exhorted followers to pray in his name, he gave them permission to ask on his behalf. They had received the revelation of God.

Second, to pray in his name means to have power with Jesus Christ. Say that a stranger comes and says, "Your son, John Mark, sent me to ask for five dollars. Here's a note from him." With this introduction, I'm more likely to respond affirmatively than if the stranger asked in his own name. When we pray in the name of Jesus Christ, we invoke him as our representative to the Father. We come to God and say, "On the basis of the merits of your son, Jesus Christ, we come to you. It's as his disciples that we ask."

Third, to pray in Christ's name also means to pray in his will. No magic formulas work here. When we ask in the name of the Lord, we are in effect saying, "This is what Christ wants." There are some areas where I can pray without hesitation. For example, I know God wants to help people—to save them, show his love toward them. I can unreservedly petition God for these things.

On the other hand, looked at this way, there are some things I can't ask so confidently. For instance, in an informal prayer meeting, a sports enthusiast prayed, "Lord, help the Astros win, in Jesus' name." My feelings were ambivalent. I appreciated his willingness to pray freely about all parts of life. (Have you noticed how we tend to pray publicly about only the "religious" areas of life?) Yet it bothered me that he could unself-consciously ask this in the name of Jesus. Would a victory by Jim's favorite team enhance the glory of God? Did God *want* the Astros to win?

I admire Jim's loyalty, but I could have better appreciated his petition if he had prayed, "Help our team to play well" or "Lord, be with the Astros."

This innocent request was relatively harmless, but people sometimes ask for selfish and even cruel results in the name of Christ. Are they trying to bring respectability to their evil and outlandish wishes?

We need to think more seriously about our requests. *Is this according to God's will? Can this help extend God's kingdom on earth? Will Jesus Christ be honored?*

Fourth, to pray in the name of our Lord means we offer ourselves to God. Jesus is our example: What he prayed, he also lived. Because he committed his life to the Father, he could say, "I and the Father are one" and "I do always the will of my Father."

To pray in the name of Christ is to pledge, "Father, as disciples we promise faithfulness and obedience. Not only do we desire to see your will done, but we also wish to be instruments to bring it about."

When we pray in the name of Jesus, we proclaim, "Jesus Christ and I are one in this request." *Dare we make such a statement lightly?*

Don't engage in magic! No tacking on! Open yourself to God honestly; make your wishes known with boldness and frankness.

I do not oppose praying in the name of Jesus; I'm only pleading for you to exercise caution before glibly saying "in his name."

Suggestions for Study and Practice

1. Do you have any prayer rituals? Do you begin a certain way? End with the same words? Do you have to be in a kneeling position? Do rituals really help you to communicate with God?

2. This week, attempt variety as you begin your prayers. Think of as many ways as possible to address God. Does this help or hinder communication with him?

3. Try praying without so much reliance upon worn terms as "in Jesus' name." Do you find it difficult? Can you pray effectively without the familiar closing?

15

Rise up and walk!

I believe in divine healing for two reasons. First, because anyone who reads the Bible finds himself confronted with the fact of divine healing. Some of the recoveries that are chronicled may be explained as psychosomatic, or even imagined—but scarcely all of them! Practically every chapter in the gospels contains healing. The book of Acts records dozens of supernatural cures. Throughout the Bible, we read, "Rise up and walk."

The second reason is a highly personal one. In 1957, my wife and I and our two daughters were driving from our home in suburban Chicago to visit my parents in Iowa for Thanksgiving. We never completed the trip. Halfway, we had a head-on collision.

I was practically unhurt. Wandalyn, my older daughter, lost a front tooth, and Cecile suffered a bruise on her knee. But Shirley was gravely injured. Her head went through the windshield, cutting the jugular vein, causing other severe lacerations, and breaking her neck. The lobe of her left ear hung by a thread of skin. Her arms were broken and pulled out of their sockets. Both kneecaps were broken. She hemorrhaged internally.

An ambulance whisked us to a hospital. The doctors spent hours sewing up Shirley. When they had patched her up the best they could, one came out and told me, "At the moment there's not much more we can do. Now we must leave her in God's hands and wait. Frankly, there seems little chance of her pulling through."

In our church back home, there was a continuous prayer chain. I called the contact person, who called three others. These, in turn, relayed my request for prayer. Within ten minutes, more than forty people were praying for Shirley.

Gus knew only that Shirley was not expected to live. He prayed earnestly for twenty minutes. In that time, God gave Gus an inner assurance Shirley would be healed.

That was Thursday. Three days later, the doctor said, "Well, Mr. Murphey, she can go home tomorrow. She's been healed—or at least she's had a remarkable recovery."

Shirley left the hospital—not in a casket, not in a wheel chair, but walking without need of assistance.

That's my second reason for believing in divine healing.

In my years of serving Jesus Christ, I've been privileged to see healings in our own family, in other homes, and on the mission field. I have seen too much *not* to believe that God heals in answer to prayer.

I am not fanatical enough to suggest, let alone to insist, that God heals in every instance; but I am serious enough and experienced enough to affirm that God answers the prayers of his people: He heals, restores, makes new.

Why does God heal? Why do I believe in healing for today?

First, God heals because he does everything to bring praise to himself. Jesus said the healing of the man born blind (John 9) was for the glory of God.

Second, God heals out of goodness, love, and compassion. Physical renewal is partial fulfillment of the promise of abundant life. Physical deliverance illustrates the relationship of the heavenly Father to his children, over whom he watches.

A friend sneeringly remarked, "If God heals, why isn't everyone healed?"

I could only reply, "Why not ask instead, 'Why is *anyone* healed?' We don't deserve it; we haven't earned it. Consider another divine activity: God saves sinners. You might ask, 'Why isn't every sinner saved?' "

God is sovereign. I cannot explain all his actions. I can only offer a few insights.

We serve the God of the miraculous. The fact that we do not always see miracles in progress does not deny their validity. (And, indeed, their absence may say something about us.)

Do we expect supernatural intervention? Many people say they don't. Isn't it possible that we "do not have, because [we] do not ask"? (James 4:2)

There seem to be two prerequisites for healing. The first is faith. In Acts 3, Peter and John encountered a lame man in the Jerusalem temple. Peter obviously had faith, for he commanded, "Rise up and walk." Immediately the man was healed. In Acts 13, Paul perceived that a certain man had faith to be healed—and he was healed. Faith must be present in either the one praying or the sick person.

A second condition is that the healing must glorify God and produce obedience in us.

A 350-pound woman asked a minister to pray for her. "I have this heart condition," she said. "My gall bladder is all messed up and may have to be removed. I think I have kidney stones, and my pituitary gland malfunctions. The doctors keep me on a rigid diet. I can't eat anything I like—and I like to eat!"

He asked, "Would you like me to pray for God to heal you so you could eat anything you want?"

"Oh, yes!" she beamed.

"Don't bother me, woman!" he said sternly. "I'll not have you on my conscience. You want healing so you can go the same way as before. You want to treat your body as a garbage heap instead of the temple of God!"

God heals that he might be praised and we might more effectively serve him. God heals that we might be aware of his power, acknowledging him as the God of life.

For months in the mission field we prayed for God to open the door to one locality where the church had made few inroads. The tribal chief finally gave us permission to start one church. "If the people want you, then we'll allow you to open more places," he said.

Henry, one of our finest national preachers, conducted the first meeting. He spoke of the God who loves and blesses people. His text was the story of the paralytic carried to Jesus by four friends.

As Henry preached, he saw a sick woman lying in front of him on a pallet. "God is here now, just as much as in the days when he walked on earth," Henry said. "Jesus Christ can heal this woman as he healed the man in the Bible."

The woman looked up at him, amazed. "You mean I can be healed?"

Henry and four of us knelt beside her and prayed. I confess the others did most of the praying, while I kept wondering what we'd do next.

The woman stood and walked! She later told us she had not walked since a childhood accident.

Because of my experiences, I have no doubt that God heals today, yet I recognize that the concept of healing baffles many. A few years ago only the small sects and fringe groups talked about it. Now we read of miraculous cures in main-line denominations.

Some advocates of healing have made absurd boasts ("God *always* heals") and have taught unsupportable assumptions ("If you don't get healed, it's because you don't believe"). While some people have gone too far in their arguments for healing, others have gone too far the other way ("Healing ended at the end of the first century" or "Healing is only for the early missionary church"). Our concept of God is too small, our requests too weak, our faith too immature. Healing is available to us—if we ask in faith, prevail in our asking, seek to glorify God, and walk in obedience to him.

I must believe in healing as long as I maintain faith in the Bible as the Word of God. In the letter of James, we read these words:

> Is any among you sick? Let him call for the elders of the church, and let them pray over him, anointing him with oil in the name of the Lord; and the prayer of faith will save the sick man, and the Lord will raise him up. (5:14–15)

I believe in doctors, vitamins, therapeutic drugs, bodily exercise, and common sense. God uses these natural processes. But I also believe in God's unlimited sovereignty. He can and does transcend natural laws and physical limitations. But belief alone is not sufficient; it must be accompanied by prayer. My rule of thumb is: Whenever anyone is sick, I pray for God's healing power. In some instances, God effects remarkable cures. In other cases, the patient doesn't improve physically (not perceptibly, anyhow), but he is certainly no worse off.

I proceed on the assumption God will heal. If he does, I rejoice. If he doesn't, I still say, "Blessed be the name of the Lord. His wisdom exceeds mine."

God's benevolence is unlimited. He provides deliverance from sin. He brings victory in the circumstances of life. Why not healing for the body?

Exercise faith. Petition God to let yourself or others rise up and walk.

Suggestions for Study and Practice

1. I have given two prerequisites for healing: (a) faith and (b) the glorification of God and obedience from man. Why are these both important?

2. This week, pray for your own health or for someone you know is sick. You may wish to read biblical accounts of healing—among them:
   Peter's mother-in-law—Matthew 8:14.
   A leper—Mark 1:41.
   Centurion's servant—Matthew 8:5.
   Jairus' daughter—Luke 8:41.
   Daughter of the Syrophoenician—Mark 7:24.
   Blind man—Mark 8:23.
   Lame man—Acts 3:7.
   Father of Publius—Acts 28:8.

3. Share with a friend or your group any insights you gain.

16

Why, God?

As our tear-strained eyes met, she blurted, "Pastor, why did she die? She worked so hard for God."

Yes, God, why? But as I squeezed Mary's hand, no helpful answer came to mind. Helen, only thirty years old, had been snatched from life. Why Helen? She was a zealous Christian worker and mother of three young boys. She was on her way to the hospital to visit a friend when her car skidded on wet pavement and smashed into a concrete abutment. "Dead on arrival," the hospital record stated.

At the funeral, many of us still struggled with the "why" question. Her husband never asked—not orally, at least, but I knew he wanted an answer. Five-year-old Timmy was less restrained: "Why did God take my mommy?"

Often in our lives, we find ourselves asking "why?"

"I know it's wrong to question God," a woman remarked, "but after we'd worked so hard and then lost our business, it's hard not to question." A friend, meaning to comfort her, said, "Down the line, God will make it all clear to us." I felt that the friend himself needed reassurance.

We envision life as happy and stable. We're geared to expect prosperity and progress. When tragedy strikes, we feel perplexed or angry. What's gone wrong? Why did this happen to *me*?

Last year, for a period of time, everything seemed to go wrong. Our family experienced an unusual amount of illness. Our church suddenly faced the trauma of attempting to minister in a transitional community; several families left the church, and I felt guilty. Also, financial problems arose.

During those weeks, I often dreaded getting up mornings. I kept crying out, "Why, God?"

In retrospect, I realize the wrongness of my attitude. If there is any common message pronounced in the New Testament, it is that *God rules*! We affirm this in our worship services: "I believe in the sovereignty of God." "I believe in God the Father almighty. . ."

God controls the affairs of men, nations, and individuals. "My times are in thy hand. . ." (Psalm 31:15) Jesus promised that not a sparrow falls to the ground without God's knowledge. (Matthew 10:29) The hairs of our heads are all numbered. (v. 30) These verses teach us God's loving message: "I care about you, so don't worry."

Isn't the real reason we ask "why?" because we don't really trust that God acts for the best? Lurking deep within us may be a fear that God has—or will—let us down. We can't reconcile our chaotic situation with his assurances of love. Yet, the scriptures abound with assurances of God's presence, protection, and love. "I will never fail you nor forsake you." (Hebrews 13:5; Joshua 1:5) The grandest promise to the believer appears in Romans 8:28–29, where Paul asserts that *everything* works for the good of God's people so that they may be conformed to the image of the Son of God.

Joseph, the favorite son of Jacob, was despised by his brothers, and one day they sold him into slavery. Joseph experienced all the heartaches of life: rejection, hatred, aloneness. But that's not the end of the story. Through the intervening hand of the Lord, Joseph became influential in Egypt, second only to Pharaoh. He sat on the throne of the world's most powerful nation at the time when Palestine withered from drought. Through his position, Joseph saved his family from starvation. Later he said to his eleven brothers, "You meant evil against me; but God meant it for good, to bring it about that many people should be kept alive, as they are today." (Genesis 50:20)

Joseph accepted life's disappointments without demanding an accounting from the Creator.

I've learned not to *insist* that God tell me why. Not because I fear to ask, or because I consider it blasphemous. God is big enough to hear my complaints, groanings, and grumblings. I still squirm, struggle, complain, moan. But now when I cry out, "God, I don't *like* what you're doing," I'm able to add, "but I accept it."

Praying that way, I believe, puts me in company with Jesus. His prayer in the garden exemplified this. "I don't want to die; I'd like another plan—nevertheless, do what *you* want."

I no longer feel it necessary for God to consult me on every issue of my life. He's the Lord; I'm the servant. We live in a world of sin and pain. The test of real Christian character is the ability to accept trials and bounce back.

For years, I assumed (quite unconsciously) that as a Christian I was at the center of God's domain. *He* revolved around *me*. He worked for my good, my perfection. I rewrote Romans 8:28: "We know that in everything God works for the blessing of Cec Murphey." But in spite of the magnitude of his love for me, God does not exist for me; rather, I exist for his benefit and pleasure. My purpose is to glorify and serve Jesus Christ, not to ask "why."

As a young Christian, I seethed with anger when I prayed and things still worked out "wrong." "Why, God?" Often, I pacified myself with, "God used this situation to teach me a lesson" or "to strengthen my faith and make me a better Christian." These interpretations, while they may be true, were rationalized for *my* sake.

I should have said, "God knows what he's doing."

God owes me nothing. Thousands of events may transpire in my life for which no explanations ever come. To parrot "We'll understand it in the by-and-by" is no answer. What if we *don't* understand it on the "other side"? Will it matter then?

The concept of God as Father helps me. I can talk to him of things that trouble me. He soothes my feelings, shares my pains, and assures me of his tender, loving care. He may explain, or he may not. If he does not, I have to acknowledge that his wisdom goes beyond mine.

When our children were first learning to walk, we had to hold their hands or they would stop; but as they grew more experienced, having us nearby was sufficiently reassuring. It's been like this with me as a maturing member of God's family. He doesn't always have to hold my hand; just knowing that he's near gives me sufficient courage to face my problems.

I no longer demand, "Why, God?" I don't need to. Instead, I'm learning to trust.

Suggestions for Study and Practice

1. When things go wrong, do you often agonize, "Why, God?" If you do, ask the reason. Are you demanding an answer from God? Is it because you resent unpleasantness and difficulties?

2. If you ask, "Why, God?" and receive no answer, can you be content? Do you feel compelled to justify God's action or inaction? Does this explain your wanting to know "why?"

3. This week, when things go wrong, practice saying, "God, I don't understand this, but you know best." Later, ask yourself if this attitude helped. Share your successes/failures with the group.

17

Which God?

Of all the proclaimers of the gospel I've heard and read, Dr. D. Martyn Lloyd-Jones reaches me as no one else does. He has shaped my theology more than any other individual. That's why I thought I must have been mistaken about what he said at the convention.

In his first message, he admonished, "Don't rush into God's presence. We seek an audience with the King of the Universe, the Lord of all Creation. We should enter into his presence reverently and with awe."

Christians are like subjects who desire counsel with the sovereign of a state, he explained. We can approach only because God decrees to hear us, and we don't rush up and embrace the king or speak in familiar terms.

He went on to say: "Jesus taught his disciples to pray, 'Our Father.' But don't any of you start thinking of God as 'Papa' or 'dear old dad.' Jesus describes God as totally different from any human father. In the churches of today, I see evidence of a familiarity creeping in. God is *not* a man. He is Totally Other. He should be addressed and respected in this manner."

Dr. Lloyd-Jones's description confused me. To me, God seemed intimate, close. My prayers had always been informal. Had I been wrong all these years? Had I been praying to the real God—or to a construct of my imagination built on sentimentality and fantasy?

Have you noticed how the views of preachers, teachers, and authors vary? Some portray the "Lover-God" of warmth, while others project the "Awesome-God" of power and knowledge. Is one view defective? If so, which? Or are both wrong? Why did my picture seem so radically different from that of Dr. Lloyd-Jones?

My question led me into retrospection. What had brought me to Christ was the realization that God loved me. It happened during a period when I felt alone, unable to solve my problems. I discovered a God who understood and cared.

My friend Harley holds a different concept. He grew up in a home where his parents showered affection on him, and as a child and youth, Harley likened God's love to the warmth of an earthly father. But in college, he experienced bitter disappointments and turned away from his religious training.

"One day," he said, "I realized God knew my wicked condition. I tried to pray but felt insignificant. 'God, why do you bother with me?' I prayed. 'Look at my weakness and rebellion.' "

This was the turning point for Harley. He grasped a new concept. "I met God the all-powerful, all-seeing, perfect, and righteous Judge. I had broken commandments and defied his laws. Mercifully, he forgave me."

How do you see God? When you pray, how do you approach God? As a caring, benevolent father—or an all-powerful potentate? Which is correct?

Dr. Lloyd-Jones' challenge led me to search the scriptures. To my amazement, I found *both* pictures supported.

Jesus and Paul, in referring to God, used the term *Abba*. This Aramaic word corresponds roughly to our "Daddy." Jesus, praying in the garden of Gethsemene, wept, "Abba,

Father, all things are possible to thee; remove this cup from me; yet not what I will, but what thou wilt." (Mark 14:36) The Son addressed the Father in intimate terms suggestive of: "Dad, you take care of this. You know what I want, but I submit to you. Do whatever you think best."

Paul, in Romans 8:15–16, uses the same word: "When we cry, 'Abba! Father!' it is the Spirit himself bearing witness with our spirit that we are children of God."

Galatians 4:6 reads, "And because you are sons, God has sent the Spirit of his Son into our hearts, crying, 'Abba! Father!' "

This pictures the intimate God. Once when I affirmed this Father image as my picture of God, a learned preacher argued, "That's not God. That's some big granddaddy, a sugar daddy, a divine errand boy, a figment of wild imagination."

I responded, "I know that this isn't all there is. I acknowledge that God is pure, all-knowing, ever-present. I'm familiar with the scriptures that say this, and I accept and appreciate their truth."

And I quoted these verses:

"I made the earth and created man upon it; it was my hands that stretched out the heavens, and I commanded all their host." (Isaiah 45:12)

"Blessed be the name of God for ever and ever, to whom belong wisdom and might. He changes times and seasons; he removes kings and sets up kings; he gives wisdom to the wise and knowledge to those who have understanding; he reveals deep and mysterious things; he knows what is in the darkness, and the light dwells with him." (Daniel 2:20–22)

"The Lord is God in heaven above and on the earth beneath; there is no other." (Deuteronomy 4:39)

"Let them know that thou alone, whose name is the Lord, art the Most High over all the earth." (Psalm 83:18)

That is not merely an Old Testament concept. Paul refers to God as "the King of ages, immortal, invisible, the only God." (I Timothy 1:17)

These verses may make some respond, "But that makes God seem cold and calculating, waiting to catch me doing something wrong—peeking around corners, seeing if I'm being good, ready to punish at every chance.'

Recently I discovered my answer to the seeming contradiction. In the opening sentence of the Lord's prayer, I found both elements present: "Our Father who art in heaven." Those six words embrace both views. When we pray, "Our Father," we speak of his nearness and intimacy. When we repeat, "who art in heaven," we think of the God beyond this world, the Transcendent One.

Last week, my son and I wrestled on the floor in a little game we play. John Mark tries to push me off the "mountain" (an imaginary line we both acknowledge). Amid much banter and giggling, we scamper around. This activity illustrates my closeness to my son. The next evening he asked, "May I spend the night with Ronnie?" I was the same father to the same son, but now our relationship had changed, and he approached me as the one in authority.

On occasion, I may flatly state, "Cecile, you may *not* go out tonight." At another time, I may put my arm around her and say, "Honey, I'm pleased you're first alto clarinet with the school band." Have we changed as persons? No. Our *relationship* has changed with the change in situation.

God allows himself to be termed Father, which is a loving form of address, but he also disciplines us. In either case, he's the God who redeems people.

When praying, I usually approach God on an intimate plane—it's my nature to strike up warm relationships rather easily; I like being close and personal. Harley, on the other hand, dares come to God only after much inner preparation. His prayers come out more formal. That's *his* nature. God understands everyone, and I'm sure he meets Harley as readily as he meets me.

Harley and I also differ in our choice of hymns. I like: "What a Friend we have in Jesus/All our sins and griefs to bear," while he prefers to sing: "Come, Thou Almighty King/Teach us Thy praise to sing/. . .Come and reign over us/Ancient of Days."

What kind of hymns do you prefer? Are you attached to "He walks with me and talks with me and tells me I am his own"? Or do you feel more like singing, "A mighty Fortress is our God, a bulwark never failing"?

When we think about it, our diversity is a blessing. I don't have to be like Martyn Lloyd-Jones or Harley or anyone else. God accepts me as I am.

When we need that loving, comforting shoulder to cry on, it's available; yet, when we come before the Perfect One in contrition, he hears our confession and forgives. It doesn't matter which aspect of God you put first, as long as you put God first.

Suggestions for Study and Practice

1. How do you conceive of God—as close and intimate, or far-off and majestic? In your praying, try both. Come to him in the intimate relationship of Father, then approach God as the Awesome One. Share your experiences with friends or a group.

2. Many hymns are prayers. Perhaps your group would like to sing several hymns of praise, petition, or intercession, and then talk about their tone and content.

3. Can you accept and appreciate people who are sincere Christians but whose concept of God is radically different from your own? Would prayer help you?

4. For a group activity, using a chalkboard or newsprint, list attributes of God. Enter these under one or the other of two headings: "Near and fatherly" and "Distant and distinct."

18

Foxes—and prayer

The gray fox knew hundreds of tricks to elude the hunters, while his companion, a brown cat, knew only one. When the hunting dogs approached, the cat single-mindedly ran up a tree, hid among the leaves, and escaped. The fox thought a long time about which of his various tricks he should employ, and while he was trying to decide, the dogs captured him.

So—what do foxes have to do with prayer? The answer is, many people know more about prayer than they can put into practice. They've learned so many tactics and strategies that they—like the fox—end up doing nothing.

Say that a daughter becomes ill and I want to pray for her. What approach do I take?

I have already described several options (chapters 3 and 4). But there are other possibilities. One is what a friend calls the "abiding prayer." She says, "I belong to Jesus Christ. I can rest in the Lord, knowing he'll take care of everything." John 15:7 provides a firm foundation for her attitude. "If you abide in me and my words abide in you, ask whatever you will, and it shall be done for you."

To *abide* means to "live" or "rest." My friend Fran quite simply takes her need to God and then rests. She shared the following incident:

"Members of our sharing group had prayed with us as the birth of our child became imminent. One couple insisted that when I went to the hospital, whether day or night, I should call them so they could pray for us. As it happened, I was rushed to the hospital for an emergency Caesarean section, and we had no time to call anyone. I'm nervous by nature, but throughout it all I remained calm. I rested in the Lord, and he sustained me. It wasn't necessary to call others."

Another way is what my friend Carl calls "praying through praise." He says, "Whenever any serious situation presents itself, I gain victory by praising God." Carl gives thanks for the situation, worshiping God for intervening in the affairs of men, joyfully recognizing divine sovereignty in all of life.

We hear of these and other prayer methods and, like the gray fox, become undecided. How do we choose the most effective way to deal with a given situation? Wouldn't it be better to know only one method?

I believe the best path is to come to God as you are, taking into consideration your temperament as the pray-er. For example, if I'm not sure God will heal my daughter, it would be hypocrisy for me to pretend to have faith and thank him in advance for an act not yet accomplished.

Another example: Different people will spend different lengths of times "praying through." Some individuals seem to "have victory" in a moment's time. (Sometimes all I actually perceive is that they've gotten stirred up. I'm not against emotions; but feeling good and having faith are not necessarily the same thing.)

A friend needed $12,000 to repay a debt, and he asked a group of us to pray with him. One man approached God by thanking him for hearing us and praising him for the answer which we were yet to receive. For me, his method "did not compute." I felt we should pray until God revealed his will, and then rejoice in the answer, whatever it was. When my turn came, I knelt and asked for direction.

The next day a Christian businessman agreed to lend the needy man the money. Had God answered one of us—both—or neither?

Another element which influences the method is the degree of personal involvement. A few months ago, I became upset over a theological issue in our church. I prayed and prayed, but no relief came. After three days I shared my concern with Shirley. "I'm pretty heavily involved," I said, "and I think my theological principle is right. Please pray with me."

When we had prayed several minutes, she said, "I know you're troubled, and I'm sorry. You're more personally involved in this issue than I am. I've prayed, but to be honest, I'm not greatly concerned about the theological implications."

There we stood. I was immersed in the issue, while she felt outside it. Her disinterest didn't prevent Shirley from sympathizing with me, but the problem necessarily remained my struggle.

On the sixth day, I knew I had finished praying. I had resolved the issue, and in the process had learned two lessons. First, I recognized that I had not been willing to reevaluate my theological position. Some doctrines, when held for many years, tend to become sacred territory not open for rethinking. I kept trying to resolve the impasse without opening myself to change. In the end, I did change. The other thing I learned was that Shirley and I, though close, didn't have the same degree of interest in everything.

Allow the Holy Spirit to lead you as you ponder how to pray. Another of Fran's experiences illustrates this principle:

"Mother went to a hospital with tuberculosis and pneumonia. Then she developed hepatitis and went into a coma. She had to be fed through the veins and after her veins collapsed, through a tube inserted in her throat.

"My brother, who was with her, called me. 'Mother won't make it, Fran. You've got to come.' I didn't know what to do. We expected our baby at any time. I called my doctor, and he forbade me to make the trip.

"I talked frankly to God. 'Lord, I can't go. I'd like to see

Mother, and I'd like for her to continue to live, but she's a Christian, and if she dies, she'll go to be with you.' I prayed as Hezekiah did when he heard he would die. I believed the Holy Spirit led me to pray that way.

"Four hours later, my brother called back. Mother had come out of the coma. She sat up, drank some juice, and talked. She has continued to improve."

That's the Holy Spirit at work.

Paul wrote, "Likewise the Spirit helps us in our weakness; for we do not know how to pray as we ought, but the Spirit himself intercedes for us with sighs too deep for words." (Romans 8:26)

If we commit ourselves to him, he will lead us to pray in the right way. There may be times for continuing to pray until assurance comes. On other occasions, we may rest in God's love and watchful care.

If you're not sure how to pray, ask God. I've often begun, "Lord, I don't know how to pray about this—lead me." Then I wait for him to communicate with me through the Holy Spirit, using as a medium my emotions, reason, or memory. I wait, knowing I will be led to pray properly. I don't always get his voice and leading, but I'm always trying to improve the lines of communication. How about you?

Suggestions for Study and Practice

1. Have you experienced times when you felt like the gray fox, confused over how to proceed? Before you pray for your own needs, or for others, pause briefly and ask the Holy Spirit to guide you in *how* to pray. Keep working on this approach until it comes naturally.

2. In your group, share a request for prayer. Ask members to take different approaches. Let some use the "abiding prayer," others "praying through praise," etc. Later, share your feelings.

19

Please listen, God

"I pray but it doesn't seem to do any good," Harold complained. "My prayers go only as high as the ceiling. What should I do next?"

Most of us experience times when we pray to the silent, hidden God, and no matter how fervently we attempt contact, we can't seem to find him. Why do we encounter periods of God's silence? Does Jesus forget his promise to be with us until the end of the world?

There are several reasons why the communication line breaks. It may simply be a matter of sin. During the first years of my Christian experience, I learned to sing, "Nothing between my soul and the Savior. . . . Nothing preventing the least of his favor. . . ." Is something between God and ourselves? It may be a sin, a wrong attitude, an unwillingness to forgive.

Once Shirley said to me, "For several days I've had a hard time in my prayers. No matter how hard I pray, it seems there's a wall separating me from God. This morning I admitted the existence of that wall—I had allowed *you* to come between the Lord and me. I had put you first." Then she smiled. "It's okay now. God's in first place again."

We must concede that God is Number One. He has declared he will allow no other gods before him. He refers not only to idols of stone and metal, but also to people, things, and ideas.

Another block in the communication line may be the lack of a systematic prayer time. A few years ago, Shirley and I bowled on a regular basis. At eight o'clock every Tuesday night, we were in position with our team. Then, with one thing and another, I found less time for this activity. Consequently, when I did bowl, my scores were poor. Why? I had lost the skill that comes from regular practice.

Practiced often and with determination, prayer becomes a natural response in times of stress or trouble. Unfaithfulness in the discipline of prayer eventually takes its toll, although the adverse effects may not be felt immediately. We can skip prayer a few days and go on momentum, but eventually we'll give out and run down. Because time elapses between the cessation of prayer and the debilitating effect, we don't always see the connection.

Overreliance on our feelings is a third barrier which may impair communication. Emotions control us far more in the field of practical religion than any other area of life.

"I don't feel like praying today."

"I'd like to touch God but he seems far away."

By relying on emotions, either positive or negative, we may miss out with God. It is by *faith* that we continue in fellowship with God.

Once for a period of seven months, my life was a vacuum. I was too "spiritual" to confess to others that God had deserted me—too dishonest to admit to myself that I prayed out of habit rather than from awareness of his presence.

I remember when the breakthrough came. On a cold November afternoon, I walked from the train station to my home. Trudging through snowdrifts over slippery sidewalks, I talked to God. "Lord, you used to give assurance of your presence. When I prayed, read the Bible, or went to church, something happened inside me—I felt alive! For months now, my emotions have been as cold as this weather."

As I railed against God's behavior, I suddenly realized he stands with us even when we are not conscious of his presence. Isaiah wrote, "Truly, thou art a God who hidest thyself, O God of Israel, the Savior." (45:15)

A resolution was born in my heart. "God, even if you never again give me any visible evidence, I'm still with you. Job said he'd trust you even if you killed him. I'm determined to do the same."

As I continued walking, I noticed that the dark clouds which had lain in the sky all day were moving away and the sun was breaking through. At the same time, the warmth of God's love broke into my being.

There are also natural physical barriers to the communicative process.

While the dentist was extracting two molars, the roots of one broke. For several days, I was miserable. I tried to read, but pain prevented concentration. I tried to pray, but couldn't keep my mind on that, either. Because my life had been ordered around daily fellowship with God, I felt undone, and I told him I did: "But, Lord, I don't want to see anyone or talk to anyone, and that includes even you. I'm too miserable to think about you, but I want you to know I love you even if I don't want to communicate."

My sense of guilt disappeared. God knew my physical limitations, and it was all right. While he yearns for our fellowship (that's the reason he created us), he doesn't demand.

The other morning I tried to pray but kept dozing off. Finally I said, "Father, forgive me. I didn't rest well last night. Conversation with you will have to come later." No guilt, no further explanation. I crawled back into bed and slept soundly for another hour.

I've written about the barriers in communication and the reasons for them. Now for some sources of relief.

Identify the barriers and deal with them. Search your heart. Is there sin? If so, straighten it out. If you come up with nothing, don't wallow in guilt feelings.

Keep trying to get through. When I fail to complete an urgent phone call, I keep trying. Communicating with God is much more important.

Remember that God wants us to pray. The Bible urges us to ask so that he can bountifully provide.

Pray in faith even when you don't "feel" like praying. Life has its stale moments.

A student may progress rapidly, then slow to a standstill. Educators call this a "plateau experience." If the student is given encouragement and support, and if he maintains his motivation or discovers new drive, he's usually able to break out of the slump and move forward again. I remember getting stuck at thirty words a minute during a typing course. I kept pecking away and one day I was shocked to find myself typing fifty-three words a minute.

If you hit a spiritual plateau, don't give up. Your wait may not be lost time; learning theorists point to the value of periods of assimilation or integration. If we're maturing spiritually, there may be times when we need to pause and let our head and heart get in stride with each other.

Don't let negative feelings derail your good prayer habits. Keep reaching and you'll come out of your slump. Tomorrow God will be close again. The surety of that relationship keeps us going.

Suggestions for Study and Practice

1. Can you recall an experience when your prayers seemed to go only as high as the ceiling? How did you resolve the sense of estrangement from God? Share this experience with the group.

2. Ask yourself, "How systematic is my devotional life? What positive steps would enable me to be more effective?"

20

It costs a lot

When my wife played the piano, it looked easy. Then I took a few lessons, and I learned there is a vast difference between banging out "Chopsticks" and playing a sonata.

Anyone can pray. But prayer skill, like musical skill, requires practice. No one prays well and with maturity by accident. He prays well who *pays* well.

The most obvious cost is *time*.

Many Christians have a God-in-an-emergency pattern of living. The world goes by, with God out there somewhere taking care of his business. Only when something goes wrong do they pray. Others give God a hurried "Good morning," a brief "Bless this food" pause at mealtime, and a modified "Now I lay me down to sleep" at bedtime. Regular but perfunctory.

To pray right means having regular times of prayer, augmented by spontaneous prayers and meditative conversations. Praying well comes by praying much—and earnestly.

Tim's responsible position demands extra hours. Last month, upon completing a difficult job, he realized he had neglected his wife and sons, and for a full week he made it a point to be home by six every evening.

The following week he confronted a task which would keep him out of town for ten days. "I'm sorry, kids," he said. "I hope you'll understand. And you know I spent a lot of time with you last week."

Ron, the older boy, blurted out, "You just stayed home those nights. You worked, or read, or watched TV. You didn't really spend the time with us."

Our devotional life can be like that. Thoughts billowing through a wandering mind aren't enough. True facility in prayer increases as undivided attention is given to Jesus Christ.

A second cost is *change*. If I ask God to mold me into the image of Jesus Christ, I can expect some drastic things to happen. I won't be the same anymore.

Harriett prayed for patience in handling her three preschool children. "They nearly drove me insane, and no matter how hard I prayed, they still got on my nerves. Then, in an idle moment, I saw 'patience' as strength to endure. I said to myself, 'Surely I can make it through today.' "

She made it through that day and thanked God for his support, and in the days that followed, she worked harder at controlling her temper and she prayed more earnestly. Soon a changed young mother was actually enjoying her children.

The apostle Paul said, "We rejoice in our sufferings, knowing that suffering produces endurance (patience), and endurance produces character, and character produces hope." (Romans 5:3,4)

Too often, we ignore the character-changing aspect of prayer. When we need help, we send an SOS to heaven. Then we wait for the answer—neatly packaged—to come bumping down the chute. We thrust the parcel under our arms and march off, tossing a "Thank you" over our shoulder. But God doesn't run a mail-order house. We have to approach him seriously and deliberately. We have to recognize that change in us may be part of the answer.

When I first became a Christian, I prayed for more faith. "God, I'm weak and filled with doubts and misgivings. Increase my faith." I hoped to experience a blustering wind from heaven, similar to the way the Holy Spirit came upon the disciples at Pentecost. I wanted to be swept off my feet and be filled with zeal and power.

I didn't experience that; instead, one trial after another came my way.

First, I was in the Navy and wanted to enter college in the fall. Because my discharge date was September 30, I applied in the spring for an early discharge on September 1. The summer began slipping by with no answer. I begged God, "Please work it out."

Meanwhile, finances snagged. Also, Shirley became pregnant and was ill for six months.

I cried to God for help, and in the end, the early discharge came through, my finances were settled, and Shirley improved. But I had paid the price for my prayers: after opening myself to change, I went through some anxious and painful growing experiences.

Faith is strengthened by confronting situations which test it. The New Testament speaks of promises to him who overcomes. Have you ever seen a victor who never fought a battle? We grow by following Jesus Christ. As we struggle and conquer, we find ourselves relying more heavily upon God's providence.

A few months ago I wanted to resign my position. "God, what are you doing to me? I hate the way things are going. I work, yet seem to get no place. Get me out of here."

A wise and loving friend said, "You're not quitting. God's not through with you in this situation."

He was right. I held out for another two months. Then one morning in my quiet time, God assured me that victory lay ahead. I got on top of my "insurmountable" problems and once again rejoiced in my work.

I grew through the experience. I felt closer to God. I also felt closer to people, for I had become more sympathetic and understanding.

I've always been a strong person. I've shrugged at problems

and, wearing a smile, have said, "That's part of the Christian life." I wasn't hurting—and I wasn't growing.

As I rethink my Christian experience, three outstanding periods of growth come to mind. In each instance, the events leading to the spurt of growth were forced upon me and were painful. Through God's enabling power, I changed in attitude and behavior. My trauma turned to triumph.

A third price for prayer skill is *determination*. Two years ago, Gerald confessed, "I don't really take time to fellowship with the Lord, and I'm going to do something about it."

Gerald meant it; yet he soon slipped back into the old grind. That didn't surprise me. I had seen him start many courses for self-improvement but stick with none of them. Gerald has a superficial acquaintance with a great many subjects but lacks expertise in any concentrated area because he has never made a determined committal.

A rich and meaningful relationship never just happens—it grows! It demands watchfulness and care. To be a praying person, you must be a determined person. Prayer isn't easy, but don't be discouraged. Start by asking God for help in making *today* a day of spiritual growth. Open yourself to him today. You'll pay, but it'll be worth it.

Suggestions for Study and Practice

1. Three costs of a more effective devotional life are time, change, and determination. Ask yourself, "Am I willing to take the time? To open myself to change? To stick to my commitment?"

2. With your group, discuss these questions: Do I really want to grow spiritually? How much am I willing to pay? Where can I draw support? How can I help others in their own quests?

21

Answer your own prayers

His first day in the mission field, Dave announced that he would not be disturbed before 11 a.m.

"I get up early, have a quick breakfast, and then it's my time for God," he said. "After eleven, I'm ready to work."

It sounded very spiritual—but it meant someone else had to do Dave's work.

"Why can't he pray at night?" asked a fellow missionary.

A co-worker demanded of Dave, "Why don't you get up three hours earlier and get your praying done? That way, you could do what you're expected to do."

Dave adamantly refused to change.

God's people pray, but prayer alone is never enough. Someone has said, "Pray as though everything depended on God; work as though everything depended on you."

I once held special services at a church in upstate New York. "We want to see our church grow," the pastor informed me. "In preparation for your coming, we've been asking God to bring people in for the services."

When I got up to speak, I asked, "How many of you would like to be able to answer your own prayers?"

Although perplexed by my question, several raised their hands.

"Okay," I said, "let's organize ourselves in teams of two and go out and visit prospects. Let's call on the apartment complexes which surround this church. We'll go *out*, and God will bring people *in*."

I got no volunteers.

Often we're willing to pray earnestly and faithfully. We're willing to let God act, but *we* don't want to *work*.

Irene had labored in India more than thirty years without furlough. She had gone as an independent missionary and lived as economically as possible. She had never asked for a cent from anyone but God. Elva, a member of our church, had met Irene on a visit to India, and they corresponded regularly. At a midweek prayer service, Elva read aloud a letter in which Irene expressed a desire to return to her native Canada, but made no request for assistance.

Elva concluded, "Irene is tired and deserves a furlough. Let's ask God to speak to people to provide her fare of about seven hundred dollars."

"I know a better way to pray," Susan spoke up. "Let's ask God to help *us* provide the money."

"But we're such a small church," someone protested. "We have only forty members."

"Remember Gideon's small army?" Susan challenged. "And David had only a slingshot. Didn't Samson kill a thousand men with only the jawbone of an ass? We can raise the money."

After the shock wore off, we prayed, and we agreed to continue to pray until God had raised the sum out of our forty members. Within three weeks, we had collected $743. Irene came home a month later.

Let's review what happened. First, we prayed. Then we got off our knees and took action.

In church circles, it's sometimes said that members fall into two categories: those who *pray* and those who *do*. The sisters who were friends of Jesus fell into these two categories. Mary wanted to sit and listen to Jesus; Martha worked in the kitchen, preparing food. Some people today use the excuse: "I'm a Mary. The Marthas can do my share of the work." This attitude betrays a misunderstanding of prayer.

True prayer is never passive. Prayer works aggressively. After Peter made his famous confession of faith ("You are the Christ, the Son of the living God"—Matthew 16:16), Jesus spoke to him about establishing the church and said, "The powers of death shall not prevail against it." Jesus trained the disciples to be militant.

Prayer is action. Praying right leads to doing right. Those who limit their petitions to "Bless Aunt Mary and Uncle Ken and bless the people of our church" *could* answer their own prayers, in part at least. They can help bless others by considerate acts. Don't throw it all on God.

At a women's meeting, an elderly lady said she could no longer stoop over, and mopping her kitchen was especially difficult. "I wish you'd pray for me to find someone who could come in and help me with a few things like that," she said. No one prayed at that time, but the next day a member of the group appeared at the lady's door and said, "Hi, there. Yesterday, you asked for someone to mop your floors. Well, I'm the answer to your prayer." This *doer* knew the secret of real prayer.

God does not do for us what we can do for ourselves. To turn to him honors God; yet to ask him for what we can do for ourselves is stupid or lazy. I would not, in my present state of good health, ask God to send someone to help paint my house. I might ask for energy or time, but I'm quite capable of doing the work myself.

In their first battle at Jericho, the Israelites won a resounding victory, but in the second battle, at the small town of Ai, they were defeated. Joshua sought an explanation:

> Then Joshua rent his clothes, and fell to the earth upon his face before the ark of the Lord until the evening, he and the elders of Israel; and they put dust on their heads. And Joshua said, "Alas, O Lord God, why hast thou brought

> this people over the Jordan at all, to give us into the hands of the Amorites, to destroy us?" . . .The Lord said to Joshua, "Arise, why have you thus fallen upon your face? Israel has sinned." (Joshua 7:6–7, 10)

From there, Joshua takes action. The guilty man is discovered and punished.

Prayer leads from self-centeredness toward openness and concern for others. If our lives are not growing outward, we need to reexamine our prayers. For example, do you want unity in your church? Then be sure you yourself are cooperative.

What are you praying about the most? Try answering your own requests by helping yourself and other people. Ask, "What can I do?"

Suggestions for Study and Practice

1. Examine your prayers. Which requests can you yourself answer? Which ones *will* you answer?

2. How often does your church or a group within it depend upon God to do things they could do for themselves? With your group, discuss ways to bring about a transition toward greater self-reliance.

22

It takes time

Ellie glanced at her watch. Although it was nearly midnight, much housework remained to be done. She felt despondent and a bit guilty. "Dear God," she prayed, "where does my time go? I never seem to get caught up."

Do you feel victimized by the clock? Some of us have dishwashers, garbage disposals, automatic washers and dryers; we have permanent-press clothes, frozen dinners, and two cars—yet, our days continue to shrink. Life should be getting simpler; instead, it grows more complicated. We ought to have more time for leisure, but is chasing around in social, educational, political, recreational, and even religious whirls "leisure"?

I'm a compulsive individual. Often people ask, "How do you get so much done?" Oddly enough, I frequently see myself as a laggard. I berate myself because I can't finish everything I've scheduled mentally.

A few among us may have more time than things to do,

but the majority want the world to stop for a few hours so we can get some rest. Yet the world continues going around . . .and around. . .and around.

I've prayed about this problem often enough. I've made resolutions either to reduce my activities or devote less time to certain commitments. I've heard that inner voice shout, "Hey, Cec, slow down!" I'm trying to listen to that voice, and I've set up several guidelines.

First, decide on priorities. Jesus knew his priorities; the first was fellowship with God. What is your foremost priority? What's second? Third?

We find time to do the things we want most. Often when we complain about lack of time, we're deceiving ourselves and others. For example, a housewife spends four hours hooked on soap operas and frets because her family has nothing to eat but frozen dinners. "I was just too pushed today," she says. Nonsense! If your first priority is soap operas—or gabbing on the telephone or frequenting the golf course—then recognizing your value system is the first step toward constructive change.

Jim remained in the ministry less than two years. "I had to get out or have a nervous breakdown," he said. "I just couldn't get any time for myself or my family."

I understood. It was Jim's nature to be the great problem solver. Every sickness, every crisis, Preacher Jim appeared on the scene.

One day a parishioner asked him, "Why do you have to play God in every situation? Can't you ever allow people to make their own decisions and solve their own problems? You're like a mother hen."

Jim didn't get the message; instead, he got angry. Only months later could he recognize the wisdom of his friend's words.

I used to think time was a problem of preachers alone. "Oh, if only I had a nine-to-five job like other people, with free weekends!" Now I recognize that other occupations have as many (or more) hazards.

"I don't know what to do," Ruth said. "I work five days a week, am involved in PTA and a women's circle, and share in a school carpool. My husband and I seldom get time to talk to each other. We have a $65,000 house where we pass each other coming and going. Is that *living*?"

A good question with an obvious answer. And setting priorities can help this situation.

Second, learn to say no. For compulsive people, that's hard, especially when there are so many opportunities for service.

A group of clergymen began a prison ministry. Bill undertook to set up the schedule and asked if I would give one day a month.

"I'd be delighted," I replied.

A few days later, I got around to praying about my decision. "Lord, guide me in this grand opportunity to affect the lives of those prisoners."

Inside, a voice demanded, "Who told you to say yes?"

"But Bill needs ministers. Think of the good we can do. And it's only one day a month."

The voice spoke again. "But did I tell *you* to get involved?"

Then I knew: Worthy project or not, God hadn't directed my action. The next day I phoned Bill and explained, "Bill, I've prayed about it and just do not feel I can squeeze it into my schedule. I'm sorry."

He understood. "Sometimes we have to realize that the rubber band stretches only so far—then it breaks," he remarked.

Third, keep evaluating. Priorities have to be reviewed and rearranged. An activity which demands our energy now may become unimportant in six months.

Review your priorities. Does your schedule include daily time spent in the presence of God? Are you allowing sufficient time for relaxation? Can you spend a few minutes or an hour doing nothing and not feel guilty? Must your hands or mind be incessantly involved in some "practical" task? What about rest? God's commandment about Sabbath observance contained two parts: First, work six days. Second, rest one day. Most of us can fulfill the first part better than the second.

"The curse on modern civilization is the clock," a businessman said. "*It* regulates *us*. We worship Father Time more than we do Father God."

Life is not to be measured in terms of distance run, but in the quality of the running. The real questions are: Does my handling of time make me a better person—a more faithful Christian? Does the way I use my time honor God?

Time is here to stay; we have to reckon with it. People like me must keep asking, "Can I learn to be more flexible? Can I ease up a bit, rest more?" Others may, on the other hand, need to ask, "God, can I learn to discipline myself and get more work done?" Either way, a review of priorities is in order.

Suggestions for Study and Practice

1. Note your priorities mentally or on paper. Ask, "God, what do you want me to put first in my life? Second?" Once the priorities have been set, keep check on yourself. Am I keeping them in perspective? Do I need to reorder them? Am I being faithful to what I know is right?

2. Can you say no to a task or position without a twenty-minute explanation? Can you say no without suffering gnawing guilt? The next few days, try to deal more positively with demands made upon your time.

3. Ask yourself, "How important is my time with God?" Share your feelings with the group.

4. Your problem may be that you drive yourself. What can you do about easing up and resting more? Or, you may be the slow starter. Ask yourself, "How can I learn to organize my time better?"

23

The will of God

"He loves me. . . . He loves me not. . . ." As Janet pulled the last petal off the daisy, she exclaimed, "He loves me! *He loves me*!" A popular game, but not very reliable.

To learn God's will, we often resort to similarly foolish exercises. A woman sticks a hatpin through her Bible, and wherever it stops becomes the word of guidance. People close their eyes, flip open the Bible, touch a page with their fingers, and the verse pointed to is supposed to show the will of God. I once tried this forecasting and got I Kings 11:3. "He had seven hundred wives, princesses, and three hundred concubines." Somehow that didn't seem God's will for me.

Tea leaves. . .horoscopes. . .fortune cookies. . . . One man writes options on slips of paper and tosses them in the air. The paper landing closest to his feet determines his course of action. Somehow I don't think this is what Jesus meant when he said, "He [the Holy Spirit] will guide you into all truth."

When I talk to a group about prayer and the question of

God's will comes up, I try to avoid dealing with this subject because so many who ask want a shortcut. They want five easy steps, or a magic formula, or an elaborate ritual for ascertaining God's will.

Of course we want to know God's will, but there is no foolproof method for extracting divine guidance. In reading the Bible as well as journals and biographies of great Christians, I've discovered no sure-fire means. Even the most devout individual lived with some uncertainty and trembling. Each made decisions by faith, and so must we.

To act in faith is to seek guidance thoughtfully and prayerfully and then do what seems best. God may speak to us through a verse in the Bible, a conversation with a friend —or not at all. To affirm, "This is God's will," is a statement of faith. We cannot objectify these experiences. It's foolish for us to insist that "this proves God is leading me."

To state, "Today is Thursday," presents no problem, because we can check the calendar and verify this fact. But to state, "The Lord wants me to quit my job," puts us in another realm. You may believe God has spoken to you, while I may attempt to dissuade you. In the final analysis, *you* take the step of faith. "Faith is the assurance of things hoped for, the conviction of things not seen." (Hebrews 11:1) What is seen, felt, touched, or empirically verified is *not* faith.

I have no magic to recommend. I give only one general principle: *Pray.*

At times God's directions have come to me plain and clear, and nothing could persuade me otherwise. At other times, I've prayed, "Lead me, Lord," only to receive no clear guidance.

During one period, the apostle Paul must have felt he would never again receive proper instructions for his ministry. Time after time, he and his followers laid strategies or actually proceeded to a place only to have the Holy Spirit turn them back. Finally, in a vision, a man of Macedonia was standing, begging Paul, "Come over to Macedonia and help us," whereupon Paul concluded this was a valid call from God and went to preach the gospel there. (Acts 16:6–10)

Don't feel undone when guidance seems obscure; eventually it will come. I would like to share three principles which I use as I try to ascertain if something is really God's will.

1. **The inner voice communicates.** I'm learning to listen. "Speak, Lord, let me know what you want of me. I'm waiting." Perhaps the answer comes in the form of thoughts —a kind of inner message from some unknown voice. I choose to believe this is the Holy Spirit speaking through human faculties. I listen to that inner voice, and often it is right, although I seldom have total assurance. A friend calls this voice "the gut-level feeling."

Once, when faced with limited time, I prayed about whom to visit. The inner voice directed me to Marge's door.

"Oh, the Lord knew when to send you," she exclaimed. "I was hoping you'd come by. I feel so depressed. Just seeing you cheers me up."

2. **Common sense makes sense.** God does not call me to a position I'm incapable of filling, whether because of temperament or lack of training. When the divine timetable called for the evangelization of Europe, who went? Peter, the uneducated fisherman? No. Paul, the educated Jew, was sent. It was Paul who argued with Greek philosophers on Mars' Hill in Athens. Paul witnessed before royalty. Learned Jewish leaders in Rome heard his presentation of the faith. God picked the man for the job and the job for the man.

If someone were to suggest that the Lord wanted me to become a mechanic or professional singer, it would make no sense and I would resist. Still, it is incumbent upon me to recognize and evaluate my gifts. When God ordered Moses to speak to Pharoah, Moses offered an excuse, but God didn't accept it:

> "Oh, my Lord, I am not eloquent, either heretofore or since thou hast spoken to thy servant; but I am slow of speech and of tongue." Then the Lord said to him, "Who has made man's mouth? Who makes him dumb, or deaf, or seeing, or blind? Is it not I, the Lord? Now therefore go, and I will be with your mouth and teach you what you shall speak." (Exodus 4:10–12)

Either Moses had no problem with words, or God made

him eloquent. Whichever, the lesson is that we have to inventory our assets and liabilities—and our potential—honestly and creatively.

3. God plans our growth. Life includes trials and unpleasantness. Within weeks of arriving in the mission field, I had been beaten and my life threatened. Floods marooned us. Yet, there was neither fear nor doubt in my heart. God had sent us there. It was his will.

Another major undertaking did not turn out so well, however. After completing seminary, I entered a Ph.D. program. I had prayed and doors had opened. First, I finished at the top of my seminary class and received a substantial scholarship. Second, I discovered I had eight months left on my veteran's educational benefits. Third, the school took only three new students in the field of New Testament, and out of a dozen applicants, I received approval.

In praying for God's will, I had set up a condition: "God, if they accept me and you clear the way financially, then I'll know this is the pathway you want me to take." But this period, which had promised to be so fulfilling, wound up being the most miserable time of my life. Previously, I had enjoyed academic work; now I dreaded each school day. I hated every minute of those months, and before the end of the first year, I dropped out. I immediately found happiness and fulfillment in another area.

What went wrong? Why did I go to school, spend all that money, waste all those months? Had I superimposed my own desire upon God's will? Had Murphey's ambitions drowned out the voice of the Holy Spirit? I don't know—and I'm not sure the answer would be helpful.

When Moses killed an Egyptian guard, perhaps he was attempting to fulfill his calling as the deliverer of the Jews. But the slaying was not God's plan. Moses fled, and the prince of Egypt found himself cast as a lowly shepherd in Midian. Later, when God decreed Moses ready to lead again, he emerged. Moses may have felt he had wasted those forty years, but had he? I doubt it. With God directing, there is never waste.

Suggestions for Study and Practice

1. Read one or more of the following suggested readings for personal study and group discussion:
   (a) *Beyond Ourselves* by Catherine Marshall. McGraw Hill, 1968. Chapter 9.
   (b) "How I Ascertain the Will of God" by George Mueller. Tract.
   (c) *A Christian's Secret of a Happy Life* by Hannah Whitall Smith. Fleming H. Revell & Co., 1957. Chapter 8.

2. Discuss with your group how these writers ascertain God's will.

3. As you seek God's will, ask yourself, "Do I really want to know? What difference will it make in my life? Am I dedicated or merely curious?"

4. Share with the group a struggle, either current or in the past, to know the will of God.

24

Changing God's mind

Lying there, his body wracked with pain because of illness and his heart heavy because of enemy threats, the king groaned. The prophet had just been in to pronounce the bad news: "Set your house in order, King Hezekiah. Your illness is terminal."

"Oh, Lord God," the king cried out, "why now? My country needs me; my people look to me for leadership. What of my family? Lord, I've always tried to serve you faithfully. Please give me at least a few years; help me to get the people through this time of enemy invasion."

Minutes later, the prophet reentered. "I've come back with a second message from the Lord," he said.

"Yes? What is it?"

"As I left here, my heart was heavy. You have been a good man, a worthy king, and I continued in prayer for you until a word came from Heaven. 'Go and say to Hezekiah that thus says the Lord, the God of David your father: I have heard your prayer, I have seen your tears. Behold, I will deliver you and this city out of the hand of the King of Assyria and I will defend this city.' "

Does this incident, reconstructed from Isaiah 38:1–6, present a problem for you? First, God declares that Hezekiah will die. Then, after the king's pleading, a second revelation cancels out the first. Hezekiah will live.

Does God change his mind? Do our prayers cause the Lord to reverse himself? This kind of about-face is found in several Old Testament passages.

The prophet Jonah, to avoid God's missionary commission, boarded a ship going in the opposite direction. He was thrown overboard and swallowed by a great fish, which deposited him on land three days later. Jonah then preached destruction to the city of Nineveh. He proclaimed, "Yet forty days and Nineveh shall be overthrown." The prophet enjoyed delivering that message, because the Assyrians of Nineveh had for centuries been enemies of God's people. But what happened? Upon hearing the curse, the people listened; they fasted and prayed for mercy. As a result, the city was not overthrown and the people survived.

The prophet sulked on a hillside, railing against God's seeming capriciousness. "This is why I hastily fled to Tarshish. I knew you were a gracious God and merciful, slow to anger, and abounding in steadfast love, and repentest of evil."

Jonah hadn't wanted to go to Nineveh because he knew God would change his mind about destroying those wicked people. And, indeed, we are told that "God repented of the evil which he had said he would do to them; and he did it not."

In Genesis 6:6,7 and I Samuel 15:11,35, the pattern is similar. First, God pronounces judgment. Next, people repent and turn to God. Third, God changes his mind.

Is God capricious—or steadfast?

We must recognize that the Jewish people envisioned God as having human characteristics. Even though they knew he was not a human being, they used anthropomorphic terms: God has a *hand* that saves, an *ear* that hears prayer, *eyes* that see men's actions, a *nose* that smells the stench of evil sacrifices. God thinks, feels, tastes, loves, hates, and angers.

This concept depicts a God who identifies with his creatures. Yahweh, Lord of the Hebrews, cares about humanity. The people weren't bringing God down to the human level; they were merely bringing him into closer spiritual proximity to man, making him accessible. The Hebrews avoided the fallacy of Greek philosophers who painted God as some abstract principle of life.

In the New Testament, God's humanity is focused in Christ Jesus. God the Father remains largely a being beyond the human world—or one who is, to use theological jargon, "wholly other."

However, the Jews' portrayal of God as having human characteristics does not explain his repentance. Some theologians have tried to play games with this. One eminent scholar says, "God *threatened* death to Hezekiah but did not *decree* it." That doesn't make sense to me. If my doctor should say, "Murphey, you have terminal cancer," I wouldn't see that as a threat—I would expect to die. And if I recovered, I could only say, "Doctor, you made a mistake." But can I say God made a mistake? No. The Lord decreed Hezekiah's death. The fact that Isaiah says it twice shows the certainty of the pronouncement. "You shall surely die." "You shall not recover." These are two different ways of saying the same thing. Not "perhaps," and not a threat. Still, Hezekiah did recover, just as the later message said he would.

The Ninevites heard the pronouncement of doom, but they realized God not only judges the guilty but also manifests mercy for those who turn from their wickedness. God heard their cries and withheld punishment. Hezekiah cried to God for mercy, relying on the Lord's providential care, and God listened. An extension of fifteen years was granted.

Does prayer change the mind of God? I don't think so. And to be practical as well as theological, I'd say that the concept that we change God will not benefit us as much as the idea that prayer may change *us*.

Nearly twenty years ago, I experienced a religious conversion. Prior to that moment—the time of my new birth through Jesus Christ—I stood, in a spiritual sense, under the impending judgment of God for my sins. The word of the Lord to me, and to everyone else outside of Christ is, "The soul that sins shall die."

As a sinner, I knew (even though I may not have acknowledged it) that punishment was my destiny and what I deserved. But when I pleaded, "Lord, forgive me," something happened. God didn't change; Cec Murphey did. I stood in a new position and in a new relationship. My repentance changed my destiny. Or, to put it in a spiritual phrase, I "turned to God." Now, instead of "The soul that sins shall die," the message is, "He who comes to me I will never cast out."

Suggestions for Study and Practice

What are the practical consequences of expecting God to change, rather than relying upon change within ourselves? Discuss this question with your group. There may be some in the group who oppose the author's view of God as an unchanging deity. They should be given an opportunity to state their views.

25

Praying for non-Christians

"God, make Lloyd miserable until he surrenders his life to you," Barry prayed. Lloyd was an "unsaved" fellow worker.

Judy petitioned, "And, Lord, show my dad that you love him. Somehow make your salvation real to him."

If we live in relationship to God, it is both our duty and privilege to pray for those outside Christ. We want to share our happiness, so we desire the conversion of acquaintances and loved ones. However, overzealousness may turn people off. Instead of leading them to Christ, it may trigger anger or rejection.

My friend Rita commented, "Until a year ago, I lived a raw life—I was the party-goer who looked for a good time, with no afterthoughts. Now Christ has changed me, and my husband doesn't understand. At first I kept trying to push Don. I'd harp, 'Honey, if you'd experience what I do, it would make such a difference to you.' Sometimes he looked at me as though I were a freak. Later, I realized I had taken the wrong approach. I'm still praying, but I'm not pushing; I'm waiting for him to show interest."

One problem is, we seem to say, "I've had a great experience. I'm on top now and you're still groveling."

"It's a form of pride," Ken said. "We like to impress people. But if we've 'got it,' we don't need to force it on somebody else—the real thing always shines through. People pay more attention to our actions than our words."

I've long been troubled over how I should deal with non-Christians. How do I pray for them? Beyond this, how do I put "walking shoes" on my prayers and take responsible action? How do I avoid suggestions of judgment? God uses human instruments, but only the Holy Spirit digs into a man's heart and convicts him of sin. It is imperative that we ask God's guidance about how to pray and how to witness.

Years ago, I had an ardent desire to "witness" to people. If I didn't stand up and speak out for the Lord at every opportunity, I felt guilty. In retrospect, I recognize I offended many people. For example, a radio counselor advised putting gospel literature around the house for the unsaved person to read, and I tried this tactic with a relative. It didn't work. He saw through my subterfuge and purposely ignored the material. I may have done more harm than good.

A real awakening came during my missionary service in Kenya. One day I went to buy some parts for my British Ford. The clerk, an Asian, wore a turban, indicating he was a Hindu. While he was filling my order, a missionary from another denomination came to the counter and we exchanged a few words.

As soon as the Hindu returned, the other missionary started to witness to him. "It's grand to have cars, isn't it? But one of these days those of us who know Jesus Christ as our Lord and Savior will fly away on clouds. Isn't that good news?"

The clerk nodded but said nothing.

Unconsciously, I joined in, giving the Hindu a full gospel plan on how to obtain eternal life. Suddenly, I stopped. Is our witness motivated out of real concern for this Hindu's soul? I wasn't sure the man's salvation was my primary focus.

I had answered questions the Hindu hadn't asked. I hadn't treated him as a person, but as an object—a soul to be won and tabulated. I had also worked hard to impress my fellow missionary. Recognizing this, I mumbled, "Sorry, I just got carried away."

"That's all right," the clerk responded. Now I saw a *human being* smiling at me.

Before we can pray effectively for a person's conversion, we need to ask, "Why am I praying? Out of duty? Out of guilt? Or do I really yearn to see this man won to God? Am I willing to do whatever God tells me to do in order to see him won?"

The first step in prayer for unsaved people is to love them. Outside of love, there are no pure motives. Statistics aren't first with God. So, let love guide. If I love a person, I won't look down on him or try to coerce him; instead, I'll be attentive to his uniqueness and his needs.

Bill, a friend, put me in my place. We had a serious disagreement, and, trying to be the noble one, I humbled myself to make reconciliation. "Sorry, Bill, I spoke out of turn," I said, following this with three minutes of self-blame.

When I finished, Bill said, "I hear your words, but I don't believe a thing you've said. You don't care about my feelings. All you care about is preserving your role as a peacemaker."

Bill was right. My concern was for my image.

Three days later (why did it take me so long?) things could be straightened out, because by then Bill's personhood had become significant to me. I could sincerely confess my failure and beg his forgiveness. He responded positively.

Let love direct your prayers, and, also, let love direct your actions. I believe that, on the unconscious level, our actions speak louder and more forcefully than all our words. In fact, sometimes our actions shout "Liar!" to our words.

While I was in Africa, a Muslim from South India became my good friend. We often drank tea together. After we had been friends more than two years, Yusufu said to me, "I am now a believer in this Jesus you teach."

This surprised me, for I had rarely spoken directly about my faith. He and I had talked of books, education, economics, customs—but we had seldom touched upon the subject of religion.

As Yusufu told of his struggles to believe, one thing that he said struck me forcefully. "You've been different from many missionaries we know. You care about people. You find happiness in your religion. I have wanted this same kind of happiness, and so I have turned to Jesus."

It's our actions which count the most. The gospels tell us that God loved the world so much that he came to earth garbed in human form. Jesus healed sick people, cast out demons, wept over his friends, took time to bless little children, and told a woman of the streets that God had forgiven her sins.

Pray and expect God to direct your prayers into action. I have no desire to attempt to tell you specifically *how* to approach each situation—I'm not the Holy Spirit. All I can say is, love people and let that love guide you. The extent of your love will determine your prayers and your actions.

Suggestions for Study and Practice

1. Reflect on the way you have prayed for and witnessed to non-Christians. Think through your motives. Were you moved by love? Sense of duty? Share your feelings and experiences with the group.

2. Is there someone you care about who does not profess faith in Jesus Christ? Begin praying for that person. Can you "answer your own prayers" in some way?

26

Prayer changes me

"I'm not interested in the church," the man said. "It's filled with hypocrites."

"Great!" said the Christian who had witnessed to him. "Come and join us. There's always room for one more."

An old joke, but significant because there is just enough truth so that it both tickles and bites. The fact that churches do contain hypocrites, phoneys, deceivers, and superficial people does not mean that churches have no power. Certainly, all members are not hypocrites. Even so, there is enough sickness to challenge us.

One of the most vindictive, vitriolic people I've known is prominent in her church and quotes scripture by chapter and verse. Yet, with the same tongue, she mangles and destroys. Do you know people like that?

One day two disciples came to Jesus, angered because the inhabitants of a Samaritan village had rebuffed them. "Those heathen didn't respond to our message," they complained.

"Jesus, command fire to fall from heaven and destroy them all."

The Lord replied, "You don't know what you're saying. You have a wrong spirit."

That was not the only time Jesus found it necessary to rebuke his disciples. They argued constantly over who would have the most eminent positions in the kingdom of God. "Who will sit at your right and at your left hand, Master?" they asked. James and John even got their mother to beg Jesus for honor to be reserved for them. At times the disciples wanted to take short-cuts to glory.

Jesus, on the other hand, knew where he stood with God the Father. Being the perfect man, created to exemplify true spirituality, he could say when praying, "Father, I know you always hear me." Who of us can dare say, "God always hears me and I'm always in right standing with him"?

True prayer involves searching our own hearts and realizing that God searches them, too. In Psalm 139, the writer is totally aware of God's presence in his life. He says over and over that he can't get away from God or fool him.

> O Lord, thou hast searched me and known me! Thou knowest when I sit down and when I rise up; thou discernest my thoughts from afar. Thou searchest out my path and my lying down, and art acquainted with all my ways. Even before a word is on my tongue, lo, O Lord, thou knowest it altogether. . . . Whither shall I go from thy Spirit? Or wither shall I flee from thy presence? (1–5,7)

He concludes with a request. "Search me, O God, and know my heart! Try me and know my thoughts! And see if there be any wicked way in me, and lead me in the way everlasting." (23–24)

This is effective praying.

In many churches I hear mumbling and grumbling:

"People don't cooperate as they should."

"A few of us have to carry the whole load."

It's easier to peek into someone else's life than to examine our own motives and values. Why am I complaining? Am I covering up, or excusing my own failure?

We can't blame others and excuse ourselves every time

things don't work out. God makes us responsible for *one* person and only one person. You are not ultimately responsible for my actions, decisions, or failures. You can be concerned—you can pray or counsel—but in the end, I am responsible to God for myself.

Still, we are human, and we often see ourselves as the only faithful Christians who really care about God and his work. There was a man like this in the Old Testament. He had been faithful, and he was outspoken in condemning evil. When persecution came, he fled from his enemies. He cried out, "God, am I the only one left in all the world who is still faithful?"

God replied to Elijah, "Stop whimpering! I have another seven thousand who aren't worshiping false gods. Stop feeling sorry for yourself and get up and move!"

Elijah prayed, and God set him straight. That's one of the main reasons I believe in prayer. God not only *knows* it all, but he *speaks*, showing us our real selves. If you're a praying Christian, you're constantly examining yourself, asking questions like, "Why did I say that? Why did I purposely hurt her?" We've all seen the motto, hung in kitchens and dens, "Prayer Changes Things." Another good motto is, "Prayer Changes People." Even better: "Prayer Changes *Me*."

Paul wrote two letters to the Corinthian church. Even though he had to correct their excesses, Paul said the people of Corinth were second to none in spiritual gifts and willingness to serve the Lord. Yet, one of his strongest exhortations is found at the end of Second Corinthians: "Examine yourselves, to see whether you are holding to your faith. Test yourselves. Do you not realize that Jesus Christ is in you?—unless indeed you fail to meet the test!" (13:5)

Are you examining your life by talking to Jesus Christ—or are you living on memories of past achievements and acts of devotion? Are you drawing nearer to God today than a year ago? Ten years ago? Yesterday?

God calls us to a continuing, ever new examination of ourselves. As we pray for others, as we surely ought, may we have the courage to pray for ourselves: "Search me, O God, and know my heart. . .and lead me in the way everlasting."

Suggestions for Study and Practice

1. Read Psalm 139 aloud in your group, remembering this is a "prayer psalm." After you have completed the reading, allow time for silent prayer in which each member asks God to search his heart. Perhaps two or three might also pray aloud for the group.

2. Can you recall experiences where God has changed your attitude through prayer? If so, share with the group.

3. This week, as you pray for others, ask God to change you, as well.

27

When people play God

Wouldn't you like to be God? Think of what it would mean to have his power, wisdom, and unlimited abilities.

Have you ever pictured yourself as the sole monarch of the universe, with everything at your disposal and command? Stories of Superman and James Bond intrigue us because they elevate a character above the normal ranks of mankind. We'd probably all like to be superior—it's a curse inherited from our original parents.

In the garden of Eden, Satan tempted Adam and Eve: "You will be wise," the serpent taunted. "You will have power; you'll be like God himself."

They listened and yielded. A little later, they were driven from the garden. They were forced out of the place of happiness because they had tried to become like God.

Being shut out of Eden didn't cure man of his rapacious ambition. We're still trying to claw our way to supernatural power and even immortality. And this is still another reason for us to pray, because in prayer the Holy Spirit discourages us from trying to play God.

Harry and his wife, Betty, were in the middle of every church activity. Then something happened and they gave up their positions of leadership. I noted their absence from several Sunday morning services.

As their pastor, how was I to respond? I visited them, always trying to find out what was wrong without directly charging, "Hey, you've turned your backs on the Lord." I prayed for them, too, and one day an inner voice spoke to me: "Who told you to play God?"

Startled, I asked, "What do you mean by that?"

"You keep asking for guidance in helping them work out their problems. Have you ever stopped to think maybe it's *their* problem and not yours?"

"Sure, Lord, but I wanted to help."

"You're deceiving yourself. You want to be the great pastor who solves everything for everyone."

"That hurt!" I told the Lord.

"Yes, I know. But Harry and Betty must work out their own struggles. Be available, love them, care about them, even pray for them. But this is their battle—theirs and mine."

"All right," I promised.

Many of us are programmed so that we like to help other people. We honestly want to help, but we don't always know where to stop. Sometimes we hinder the cause of Jesus Christ. We try to straighten out our fellow adults. We force children to live by our commitments rather than supporting them as they make their own.

Listen to us:

"I've told Ethel a hundred times she ought to leave that louse and divorce him."

"I'm telling you this for your own good, Arnold."

God calls us to help one another, and that means caring. But our love is to be a sensitive love—we are to care about others as we care about ourselves. Sometimes caring means hands off. Sometimes loving means allowing an individual to make mistakes.

The McQuillans were married ten years before they had

their first child. It's surprising to me that Deborah managed to grow up, for she was the most protected child I ever saw. When she was learning to walk, her mother hovered around her. To be sure she never contacted germs, Mrs. McQuillan seemed forever spraying the house with Lysol. At night, she got up two or three times to see that her baby was covered with blankets.

At age eighteen, Deborah left home. "It was the best thing I ever did," she remarked later. "Until now, I've never lived my own life or made my decisions. My parents did everything for me, and I behaved the way they wanted. I had no childhood; I was a puppet on a string."

Deborah had to free herself to make her own mistakes, to learn, to grow.

Have you ever felt the pressure of someone playing God in your life? A parent—child—spouse—friend? He tried to force you into a decision when you weren't convinced. He quoted scripture to point out your responsibilities and duties. Even when he was right, you resisted conforming to *his* opinion. You felt resentful. I know I've pushed people in the direction I believed was right, and I've even resented it when they didn't follow my advice. But suppose my suggestions had led them astray. Would that have made me happy?

There are problems which only God can work out. Jesus knew how far to go with a man. He knew Judas would betray him, yet the Lord didn't exhort, "Judas, repent and get right—or else!" Jesus loved the man. At the very moment of betrayal, Jesus looked into the eyes of that demon-filled disciple and said with sincerity, "Friend."

Jesus set the example. He cared, but he allowed a man to make his own choices. We smugly assume that all the answers are in our hands. We want other people to be dependent upon us. How different from Jesus, who said, "The Son of man sets you free."

Suggestions for Study and Practice

1. Ask yourself, "Am I trying to play God?" Examine your relationship with your husband/wife, children/parents, friends. Share with your group. Ask them to pray with you and for you as you work to improve these relationships.

2. Is there someone trying to play God in your life? Pray for this person.

28

Give up?

"Lord, I haven't meant to disobey," I confessed. The issue wasn't important, but my deliberate and continuing evasion of it was.

"I'm so weak. Please help me in my weakness," I pleaded.

"No, that's not true. The trouble is, you're too *strong*."

"Too strong?"

"Yes, too strong in your own way. As long as you are determined to do as you please, I can't help you."

By nature, I'm self-reliant. My experiences have led me to embrace and espouse rugged individualism. I'm inclined to think that I need no one, that I can do everything for myself.

That's the opposite of what Jesus teaches. Our trouble is, we're strong in asserting our own will, but weak in following his teaching. When we realize this shortcoming, the power of Jesus Christ can operate in our lives.

This principle became clear to me as a young father. Shirley woke up with a splitting headache and nausea. The baby,

John Mark, had colic. The two girls, having just gotten over the chicken pox, were fussy. In spite of all this, the day didn't start out too badly for me. I made breakfast, washed dishes, swept the floor, got the baby calmed down. But later everything started to go wrong. The girls demanded ice cream, but when I served it, they refused to eat it. They hit each other and argued over who started it all. This woke up the baby, who howled. A new wave of nausea attacked Shirley.

By midafternoon, I felt like screaming. Instead, I prayed. "Father, I'm at the end of my rope. I can't do anything right, and my nerves are shot. Please, please help me."

A calmness came over me. The girls, who had been throwing blocks at each other, suddenly stopped and lay down for a nap (an unheard-of occurrence). Baby John Mark also slept peacefully. Shirley came downstairs and announced, "I'm feeling fine now."

In my state of helplessness, God had intervened. But why did he allow me to go through those nervewracking hours? I don't know, but when I gave up, God gave.

A few weeks ago, I talked about "prayers of helplessness" to a sharing group. Betty listened intently, then said, "Oh, that helps so much. I've always heard, 'God helps those who help themselves.' We ought to say also that 'God helps those who can't help themselves.' "

I become angry at myself when I realize how many times I've refused to admit my helplessness and God's strength. Belatedly, I have to say, "Forgive me for thinking I could do it all. I keep forgetting how much I need your help."

When we first began to work among the Luo and Suba tribes, we made little progress. Our area had been in turmoil. Several of our national evangelists became discouraged and quit. Recognizing that revival was the answer, I tried to promote an awakening through big outdoor meetings, visitation from village to village, distribution of tracts by the thousands, exhorting local Christians to be more fervent. These activities were not bad in themselves. The difficulty was, I tried to bring in the awakening instead of letting it come from the Lord.

In a discouraged moment, I said to the African overseer,

"We've tried everything. No matter what we do, it doesn't seem to work. The only thing left is concentrated prayer."

For weeks we prayed every morning, beginning at six o'clock and continuing for an hour, reminding God (mostly ourselves) that Jesus Christ is Lord of the harvest and we are only the laborers—that we work, but God produces the results. Revival came in answer to our "prayer of helplessness."

One of the strongest men in the Old Testament is Jacob. He got what he wanted, regardless of the method. He desired cattle (a sign of wealth) and found ways of owning a large herd. He out-deceived his deceptive father-in-law. By tricks and wiles, he always came out on top.

Then one night Jacob met God and they wrestled. Jacob lost that fight and went away limping, but he gained more than he lost. We read no more of the deceptive Jacob, who won by sheer cunning. He becomes God's man with a new name, Israel, meaning "a prince with God."

Saul, the faithful proclaimer of orthodox Judaism, persecuted heretics, pursuing them all the way to Damascus. One day this strong man fell blinded on the roadside, and another person had to lead him about as a child. The erudite, strong-willed religious zealot finally prayed, "Lord, what would you have me to do?"

The prayer of helplessness. The prayer of "giving up." That's what God requires before he can take over.

On the other hand, he doesn't want us to sit around and do nothing (a veiled excuse for laziness). His call is to those who "labor and are heavy laden" and need rest. His call is to those who work but make no progress. He calls the strong to "give up," to surrender, that they might realize their real need lies in Jesus Christ.

Suggestions for Study and Practice

1. Have you "given up"? Recall incidents when you prayed "the prayer of helplessness." What lessons did you learn from the experience? Share these with the group.

2. In this chapter, Jacob and Paul are shown as having to come to the place of helplessness before God could use them. There are others in the Bible, including Moses, Samson, and Peter. Choose one person and try to identify with him. Share your feelings with the group. Start with "I identify with____________ because______________."

29

Be thankful for the unpleasant

"I got so tired of hearing myself grumble about everything, I decided to seek a radical cure," Suzanne told our sharing group. "I tried to write down everything I was unhappy about. I wound up with 26 'miseries.' Then I went down the list item by item, giving God thanks for each of them. A few almost defeated me, but eventually I was able to thank God even for these."

A fellow member scoffed, "There are things I could *never* thank God for."

Another replied, "I can follow Suzanne—to a point. The apostle Paul says that in everything—that is, in every circumstance—we should give thanks. I can thank God for his presence when I'm having trouble—but praise the Lord for *everything*? Can you thank God for the sin in your life?"

Suzanne pondered a moment, then beamed. "Sure I can. It's through sin that I experience God's redeeming love."

The group never reached unanimity, but together we did

grapple with some significant questions: How do we handle difficult situations and difficult people? There seems to be no way of deliverance. How do we cope? How do we experience Paul's certainty, "Thanks be to God who gives us victory through our Lord Jesus Christ"? How do we live with exhortations like, "Rejoice in the Lord always"?

Suzanne's testimony keeps coming back to me. I've not reached the place where I actually give thanks for unpleasant situations, but I am getting closer to accepting and rejoicing in God's presence in the midst of crisis.

To rejoice at adversity tests the reality of our faith. Is God really with us? Is the Lord making good things happen in our lives through these unpleasant experiences? These questions must be wrestled with.

One summer I took a group of teen-age boys from our church to Mexico. For two weeks we visited churches and participated in mission activities. On our way home, the power steering of our leased station wagon became increasingly difficult to handle. Twenty miles south of Baton Rouge, the steering went out completely while I was driving nearly seventy miles an hour. The wagon crashed against the guardrail on the median and bounced back. Then it plowed into the railing again, jumped it, and landed facing oncoming traffic. The car was badly damaged, but no one was hurt.

For a couple of minutes, I sat with my head against the steering wheel, feeling sorry for us and wondering what to do next. How would we get back to Atlanta? I felt a hand on my shoulder and one of the boys said, "Rejoice, preacher! Give thanks! We're not hurt and the Lord's with us!"

I heard his words but didn't move.

"That's what you're always teaching us," he persisted. "We're okay and the accident wasn't your fault. Let's just praise the Lord for sparing us all."

He was right, of course. We couldn't undo the accident. And although we were stranded, we were not forsaken. My first impulse had been to upbraid the Lord (after all, we disciples had been about his work), but my young friend's witness made me realize that God has never promised us a rose garden merely because we are Christians. In fact, one of the ways we honor Jesus Christ is by our steadfastness in the midst of crisis.

Anyone can talk about faith; the real test is living in the face of overpowering opposition. That's the time to see how sincerely we trust and how faithfully we "rejoice always." I wish I were spiritually strong enough to worship always—even in the midst of trials. I'm trying!

Following the accident, several other incidents gave us the opportunity to thank God. Half a mile away, we found a cafe and gas station where we got food and made telephone calls arranging to pick up another car in Baton Rouge. Meanwhile, a truck came in and the driver volunteered to take us into town.

The Lord continues to teach me about rejoicing and being thankful in everything. A Yankee friend moved South with his company. After two years, the company folded and he, being a specialist in a restricted field, was stranded. When I went to console him, I found him smiling. This was strange, I thought to myself, because I hadn't begun to help him yet.

"You know, Cec," he said, "this is another opportunity to call on God."

"I'm delighted to hear you talk like that."

"I prayed about coming here for this job, recognizing there was insecurity in it. But it's O.K., because my wife and I felt definitely led by the Lord. Now it's his problem, isn't it? He led us into this, and he'll lead us out."

A few weeks later, a better job—one with built-in security—opened up for him.

Trials, frustrations, personality conflicts—we can't prevent them, but we can do something about the way we are affected. Paul spells it out like this: "Have no anxiety about anything, but in everything by prayer and supplication *with thanksgiving* [italics mine] let your requests be made known to God. And the peace of God, which passes all understanding, will keep your hearts and your minds in Christ Jesus." (Philippians 4:6–7)

The next time problems engulf you, include these elements in your meditation:

God is with me always, and he's not going to fail. Solomon said, "Blessed be the Lord who has given rest to his people Israel, according to all that he promised; not one word has failed of all his good promise." (I Kings 8:56) And Jesus assures me, "I am with you always." (Matthew 28:20)

God uses adverse situations to make me trust him for more difficult steps ahead. Nothing just "happens" to God's people. Every step strengthens our trust; we see that God is reaching out and saying, "Don't be afraid to trust a little more."

God wants me to be victorious. Paul advised the Thessalonians, "I don't want you to mourn like the heathen, for they have no hope when they die." (free translation of I Thessalonians 4:13)

How can I sum it all up? There are two words which enable us to rejoice in every circumstance: *God cares.*

Do you believe that? Rejoice! Lift up your heads and give praise. The omnipotent Creator of heaven and earth cares about puny beings like you and me.

Hallelujah!

Suggestions for Study and Practice

1. Do you tire of grumbling? When you discover yourself starting to complain, see if you can't find something in the distressing situation to thank God for. Share your experiences with the group.

2. In the conclusion of this chapter are three elements for use in meditations. When you start to worry or become discouraged, say these sentences aloud. Share your experiences with your group.

30

It ain't finished yet

Nine-year-old Judy's face beamed as she carefully selected her poster paints, poured small amounts in plastic cups, and carried them back to her worktable. Industriously, she spread yellow, red, and orange across the top of her paper. Then, beginning in the lower left corner, she splashed on streaks of green, brown, and purple.

I was substituting for the third-grade teacher and the assignment for art period was, "Paint a picture of what summer means to you."

Judy hummed as she worked.

"The colors are beautiful, Judy," I volunteered, "but what are you painting?"

She cocked her eyebrow and answered indignantly, "Who knows what it'll be? It ain't finished yet."

"Yes, Judy," I persisted, "but you were to paint what summer means to you."

"Oh, *that*," she chuckled. "Well, if this turns out to be a picture of summer, then I'll explain it to you." She resumed humming and splashing.

Judy, at nine, is immature, and her lack of direction can be smiled at and excused. But what of adult Christians who seem to have no direction? "Whatever will be, will be," they say, shrugging. Whatever turns up on the canvas of life is O.K.

I seriously doubt that such lives honor God or afford fulfillment. Decisiveness in daily living speaks positively of who we are, and of the role God plays.

The other extreme in life is Terry, who came to me for premarital counseling. I asked about his goals in life. "Oh, I have it all worked out," he asserted. "I graduate from college this June. Then I shall enter graduate school and spend three years on my Ph.D. With that, I can get the kind of job I want, teaching in a university. Donna and I will have two children, but not until I'm through with my graduate studies. Meantime, Donna will work, and we'll save for the down payment on our house. . . ."

Terry had his life all planned out.

"You've done a lot of thinking ahead," I observed, "but where does God fit into this snug picture?" Terry seemed uncomfortable. He had allotted nothing special for God. Yet, he protested, "Oh, I believe in God, all right."

Real prayers—the significant, meaningful ones—begin with a vision, a dream, a goal. To say it more theologically, the life of a true Christian begins with a commitment.

A life given to God is not one thrown at his feet and left there for him to use any way he chooses. Commitment means dedication to God and his service, but because we are all unique beings, God uses us where we have talents—that is, *if* we allow him to use us.

Marlin is twenty-nine. While discussing his future, he laughingly prefaced a statement with, "When I grow up. . ." He revealed more than he intended. Although nearly thirty, he has no goals. "I pray for the Lord to guide me, but nothing seems to develop."

Marlin made an initial dedication of his life to God years ago. Dedication to Christ, however, is never a single, once-for-all-eternity event. A Christian life begins with that initial commitment; it lives by faithfulness to that commitment.

The ideal life, as I envision it, blends planning with dreaming. We give ourselves to God as the first step. Then God hands our lives back and says, "Get on with your planning." Life can't be all free-wheeling; it has to have direction.

How does God speak to you about your personal destiny here on earth?

I became a Christian while in the Navy. From the first, I knew the call of God was upon me to preach. I had no preparation and doubted my ability. Yet, a sense of God's direction shaped my decision. After my discharge, I went to college under the G.I. Bill of Rights. I have been an ordained minister fourteen years. I am fulfilling my dream.

A college classmate had a similar vision. Alvin and I prayed together one day, and afterwards he said, "Cec, I want to preach more than anything else in the world."

"Keep working at it," I urged.

From that time on, Alvin and I prayed many times about his future.

I haven't seen Alvin in ten years. The last I heard, he was a salesman in a large corporation. There's nothing wrong with that vocation, and it may be the most valid route for Alvin to find fulfillment. It may be what God intended. But I feel a sense of personal loss when I think of Alvin's glowing face as he shared his career plans with me and then consider the possibility that he either copped out or was squeezed out of becoming the great minister I thought he could become.

I know how difficult the road to fulfillment can be. After two years of college, my finances were strained. We had a daughter and expected a second child. Shirley had to make many sacrifices in order for me to stay in school. But we felt this was what God called us to do, and we kept going. Now we know that the hardships were worthwhile.

Temptations have continued to present themselves. There was a job offer to manage a hotel chain in South America at three times my present salary. The working conditions were ideal—I could even do missionary work part time. But after prayer, Shirley and I said, "No, God didn't call us to that work. We have something else he wants us to do."

Let me stress here that God doesn't call only clergymen. He calls each of us—engineers, salesmen, doctors, housewives.

Do you have a dream? A vision for your life? What does God want?

Pug, with his brother, operates a successful contracting firm. These men give liberally of their finances, time, and abilities. Pug teaches Sunday school, leads singing in the evening service, and coaches Little League in the summer. Once he told me, "I can't preach and probably don't teach very well, but I'll tell you this, preacher. You keep up your end and give us all you've got in spiritual things, and I'll be behind you in the material."

I asked, "Pug, what kind of goal do you have for your life? Have you ever prayed about it?"

"Sure have," he affirmed. "The Lord made me able to work with my hands, and I'm a good construction man. I want to build the best buildings I can for God."

Pug knew what it meant to live out a commitment. To presevere means "praying always with all prayer and supplication." (Philippians 4:6) Fulfillment requires the continuing reevaluation of our goal, checking periodically to see how closely we conform, and frequently renewing our commitment.

No builder starts a house without plans and then watches idly to see how it turns out. No writer types words at random hoping to produce a novel. Unlike little Judy, no real painter throws paint on canvas only to determine later what the picture will be.

Do you ask God for his will for your life—both in the immediate circumstances and over the long range? He probably won't map out the details, but he'll give you a sense of direction for the investment of your energies and abilities.

I have some unfulfilled dreams in my life. A few of them are pure fantasy and will never come to fruition. Others, I pray about and work earnestly toward fulfilling.

I don't know the outcome of my life, but I have a sense of direction, a commitment to God. "It ain't finished yet," as little Judy said of her painting, but I'm sure that God knows "what it'll be." I know where I started and where I'm headed. By God's grace, I shall continue, seeking his will through prayer, until his plan for my life is complete.

Suggestions for Study and Practice

1. Which kind of person do you tend to be: the let-come-what-may type, or one who plans every detail? Do you effectively mix dreaming with planning? Share with the group, "I am a person who————."

2. This week, ask yourself: Who am I? What goal do I have for my life? Am I moving closer to that goal? Seek answers prayerfully. Share any insights with your group.

RECOMMENDED READING

Bounds, E. M. *Purpose in Prayer*. Chicago: Moody Press, undated.

Coburn, John B. *Prayer and Personal Religion*. Philadelphia: Westminster Press, 1957.

Laubach, Frank C. *Letters by a Modern Mystic*. Old Tappan, N.J.: Fleming H. Revell Co., 1958.

Lawrence, Brother. *The Practice of the Presence of God*. Old Tappan, N.J.: Fleming H. Revell Co., 1895.

Johnson, Ben C. *Learning to Pray*. Rev. ed. Atlanta: Forum House, Inc., 1972.

Parker, William R., and St. Johns, Elaine. *Prayer Can Change Your Life*. Englewood Cliffs, N.J.: Prentice-Hall, Inc., 1957.

Rinker, Rosalind. *Prayer: Conversing with God*. Grand Rapids, Mich.: Zondervan Books, 1959.

Shedd, Charlie W. *How to Develop a Praying Church*. Nashville, Tenn.: Abingdon Press, 1964.